I met her and
solis[?]

Mexican Rhapsody

Music, Madness, Magic

Laurie Saunders Rodriguez

Self-published in September 2021

*To all who have loved me, and all who have
allowed me to love them.*

1975

MEXICO

*How true it is that our destinies are decided by nothings…
a small imprudence helped by some insignificant
accident… - Henri Frédéric Amiel*

He tried to kill me before. That time, I was walking home,
crossing the frozen parking lot in front of the university
music building. It was midnight and the streetlights
beamed down on a red Impala, snaking into the lot. The
car sped towards me, a few feet away braking and sliding
out of control. I ran back towards the safety of the
building, slipping until I reached knee-deep snow, ragged
panting from behind closing in. Then, he grabbed my hair
and pushed me down, mashing my face in the ice. "This is
how you make me feel," he said. "Why won't you answer
my calls?"

"I can't breathe," I cried.

Finally, he let me go, said he was sorry. Could he take
me home?

1

I didn't tell my family. I want independence from my parents' suffocating control but I don't even know how to choose my friends or break off a relationship.

The parking lot incident was bad enough but tonight he snapped, attacked me with scissors. Sobbing, I call my dad. "I'll be right there." He doesn't ask questions on the ride home, but oncoming headlights reveal a clenched jaw and wide, focused eyes. Blood dripping from my arm soaks my white shirt scarlet. "You need stitches," he says.

The next day my dad brings home a brochure: Junior Year Abroad in Mexico. "You need to get away from that maniac boyfriend," he says. I hope he doesn't find me.

It's my dad's idea to drive me 3,000 miles to the Mexican capital, even though I prefer flying down with the other 35 students, who've signed up for the program. Dad's love affair with Mexico still rages and his vagabond spirit craves to be on the road again. My sister Ana,18 and brother George,15 will come along as well. My other five siblings will sweat out the summer at home in New Jersey.

Dad converts the back of a lime-green Volkswagen bus into bunk beds, with the heads facing front, the upper bunk a pillow's width farther back, allowing for fresh-air breathing below. For most of the trip, two of us sprawl on the upper bunk and one rides shotgun, hot, dry air blowing in from all sides through the open windows. No seatbelts in sight.

Two weeks after leaving New Jersey we cross the Rio Grande River into Mexico. That's easy enough. You don't need special documents to visit the border town, but we're going on to Mexico City and need a car permit and tourist papers.

There's no air-conditioning in the office; it's a dry sauna, even the filing cabinets are too hot to touch. A uniformed man sits behind a white, Formica-topped counter piled with papers. He pecks with one finger on an old typewriter and, without looking up, mumbles.

"He wants us to take a seat," Dad says, pointing to six white, scuffed plastic chairs lined up against the wall. There are no other permit seekers, yet we wait. And wait. Uniformed men, with slicked, jet-black hair come and go. One rushes by trailing the heavenly scent of steaming, corn-leaf-wrapped tamales and Cokes, no clue that it's way past our lunch hour and we're drooling. Finally, typewriter-man stands, wipes his hands on his pants and motions for me to accompany him to a small office. Little beads of sweat roll down my back and temples. A small, rotating fan in the glass-walled office blows stuffy noontime air around. I shrug and shake my head at the officer's questions. *"No comprendo,"* I don't understand. He raises his voice and waves his arms towards the door. Finally, my face red- hot, my heart pounding, I cover my face with my hands and weep. He stops, the whirring of the fan calming. After a moment, the tirade is over. *"Pásele,"* the officer says softly, opening the door and bowing. I return to the plastic chairs; documents soon appear and we're free to go.

"Not so fast," another uniform says, poking his head in Dad's window as we exit the walled-in parking lot. "I can take those papers away if I want."

"Thanks for your help," Dad says, pressing a few coins into his palm, and winking at me. "This is *la mordida*, the bribe, a negotiating tool. It gets things rolling."

"We should have slipped a few bills to typewriter-man

hours ago if that's how they do things here," I say.

Nuevo Laredo streets are narrow and dusty, only main roads are paved. The smell of tortillas, exhaust, and garbage fills the air. There are no signs pointing to Mexico City. Dad is unruffled, thrilled to show off his expertise in Spanish, poking his head out the window and asking strangers for directions. But no one, it seems, has ever left this town.

"That guy back there told us it was this way and now this lady says to go back. Why don't they just tell us they don't know?" I say.

"They don't want to disappoint us," Dad says. "They want us to feel welcome."

We finally find the narrow highway south. In the distance, on either side, across the vast, cactus-dotted desert, sit magnificent blue-green mountains: The Sierra Madre.

Besides the bribes and fake directions, there are lots of other clues that we're not in New Jersey anymore. "PRESIDENTE LUIS ECHEVERÍA" is everywhere, letters as large as the walls of homes and businesses permit. At every stream women pound laundry on rocks, children laughing and splashing around them, colorful clothes drying on nearby bushes. Each time we stop for gas, dirty barefoot children beg for coins. Water from spigots is not potable, and bottled water nonexistent, so we guzzle Cokes. (Mom would be horrified!) A few gas stations have bathrooms, but they're foul: no toilet seats, no water, no toilet paper, and dirty papers litter the stalls.

Dad refuses to drive at night. "Loose livestock and giant potholes all over the place," he says as we wait for a herd of cattle to cross the highway. "Can you imagine in the dark?" So, every evening, as dusk approaches, Dad looks for a private house, knocks, and asks if we can park in the yard overnight. People always say yes, even invite us for breakfast.

The only time we're turned away is at a Catholic church. "You'd best be on your way," the priest says, through the iron, padlocked gate. "Church policy doesn't allow for overnight visitors."

One foggy midnight we cruise into Mexico City on the *Periferico*, a four-lane highway with no shoulder, no extra lanes for onramps, and no speed limit. Dad clicks on the radio and the second movement of Beethoven's 5th Symphony washes over us.

"I hope I can play that someday," I say.

"This is an omen," Dad says. "I can feel it."

The second day in Mexico City, we visit the University of Mexico, where I'll be taking classes. The giant stadium was built for the 1968 Olympics and the library I recognize from the cover of my fifth-grade geography textbook: a giant mural, made from colored stones, depicting the history of Mexico.

I sigh. It's light years from New Jersey. The maniac will never find me here.

1975

A NEW LIFE

*Adapt or perish, now as ever, is nature's inexcusable
imperative. - H.G. Wells*

The thirty other students arrive in late August
accompanied by a director and her assistant. They all
know each other from their university and are a cliquish
bunch. At our first meeting no one even says hello to me.
I'm invisible.

We're assigned in pairs to different private homes
where, supposedly, we'll learn Spanish from the families.
The assistant director takes me aside to ask if I mind
rooming with a Black girl, Verna. Why would I mind?

Our hostess is a grey-haired, angry-faced woman with
three teenage daughters. The girls ignore us and our meals
are served in a separate room from the family.

"Maybe Mom thinks we'll contaminate her daughters
with our wicked American ways, " Verna laughs. "Nice
single girls don't run around unchaperoned, much less

study at university."

We try to be flexible, to adapt to new customs, or at least honor them, but it's not easy. We need to request hot water an hour before bathing, there are no towels or toilet paper, and ten people share the bathroom. Over time, other things bother me, like the lock on the telephone, the unabashed blatant lack of trust. Curfew is 10:00 P.M. because the keys they give us don't work. Why even pretend? The house is on Avenida Insurgentes, a four-lane traffic-jam, cars honking and sirens blaring day and night.

LAURIE AND VERNA

Our classes are in the morning at the UNAM, the largest university in Central and South America. My group is then free to study and meet up at local bars after lunch. But instead, I hop on a bus and arrive an hour later at the National Music Conservatory, where private violin lessons and orchestra rehearsals fill my afternoons. I feel at home with instrument-carrying students scrambling to meet me, but bristle at their clumsy hugs and kisses. I'm an exotic curio and realize that with this constant barrage of local lingo, I 'll be yacking away in Spanish before my colleagues can conjugate the verb *entender,* to understand.

A few weeks into the semester, I meet Norma, a beautiful Filipino woman who lives close by with her American husband and their two kids. David is manager of the 7 Up Company in Latin America and travel is his life. He thinks we could be a perfect match: we need a welcoming place to live and Norma could use some English conversation on the long stretches while he is away.

Their house is a Spanish, colonial-style mansion, the 10-foot wooden doors at the entrance, stone-slab floors, and chandeliers taken from crumbling 16th century convents and churches. Exotic wild animals are everywhere; skins scattered over polished wooden floors, and mournful glass eyes gazing from mounted heads.

Verna and I move into a private room at Norma's, with warm water on call and a balcony overlooking a bougainvillea-lush, palm tree garden. From our second story suite we can peek over the wall into the neighbor's muddy yard, barefoot kids running amidst loose chickens and abandoned cars. Laughing innocence thriving like honeysuckle in an overgrown junkyard.

Chamber orchestra at the conservatory is sublime. We rehearse on the wooden-floored concert stage, the lights casting halos above the six cellos and the pair of

CENTER COURTYARD AT NORMA'S

double basses, an ethereal glow emanating from the 11
violins surrounding me. We are blessed with Leopoldo
Tellez, cellist of the Trio México, as director. He knows
what repertoire will drive classical-music audiences wild
on our tours throughout Mexico. We sound like the
Chicago Symphony. I'm in string-orchestra heaven.

I'm also battling the language, still in the trenches,
hoping to get an offensive mounted soon. Either I
communicate in Spanish or I miss concert dates and go
hungry. My friends mimic my accent and howl at my
mistakes, especially the time I say *Estoy embarazada*,

thinking, "I'm embarrassed," but actually saying "I'm pregnant."

On the metro and bus system I get a taste of the best and worst of my host country. One afternoon, I ask a girl, about my age, walking towards me with an armful of books, for directions. Lupita chatters as she walks me to the metro station and then, at the entrance to the trains, asks me home for lunch. *Mi casa* and *para comer,* I understand. *Los abuelitos* (Grandparents)*, Tio* Pancho and *Tia* Juanita, *hermano* Jose and *hermanas* Gloria and Clara all show up. This is a Tuesday in September, not Thanksgiving. A four-course meal of vegetable soup, salad, *enchiladas* and jello dessert evolves into coffee hour, time to chat and catch up: *sobremesa.* I feel like a Hollywood celebrity, desperately trying to grasp a word or phrase as the paparazzi chatter swirls around me.

Another day, standing on a bus, grasping a horizontal metal pole above my head, a crowd swells on. Bodies press in. I can't move. A man is at my back, hips thrusting. People shake their heads and scold him in words I don't recognize. We're suffocating from sweat and stench. I close my eyes as tears thread down my cheek. I can feel his hardness against me and hold my breath. The bus stops, the crowd pushes off, and he's gone. Nothing happened, yet I feel humiliated. He had no right.

And then I have head lice. Norma says I got them riding public transportation or at the movies. "Just by leaning back in a seat you'll pick them up," she says, as if that makes it OK. "They even jump from head to head. We all need to use a special soap and wash all your clothes, sheets and pillowcases."

"How embarrassing," I say.

"Everybody gets them, sooner or later," she says.

"I never had them before."

"They're everywhere," she says. "You just never went anywhere."

It's my 20th birthday week and something is wrong. Bleeding for two months now, I'm exhausted. When I tell Norma, she calls and makes an appointment with her gynecologist.

"He was the chief doctor at the 1968 Olympics," she says. He should be good.

Norma's doctor tells me I have a cyst the size of a grapefruit on my left ovary and need an operation. "Another opinion is what I need," I say. The second doctor confirms the diagnosis, adding that surgery is urgent.

Neither of my parents can come to Mexico, so they send Christie, my older sister.

The anesthesia is supposed to last two hours, but I'm unconscious for ten. I can't come out. A horrible whirlpool, buzzing in my head, trembling, deeper and deeper it drags me. I can't free myself.

When I finally awake, I'm in a recovery room, surrounded by snoring women. I watch as the woman in the next bed turns over and drops to the floor. She moans as several nurses rush to lift her back onto the bed. They snap at each other; someone forgot to replace the bed rails. I vomit black fluid onto the sheet. It spills onto the floor.

The next morning, my doctor arrives smiling. Not only have they removed the grapefruit-sized cyst on the left side, but one from the right also. "And since it was in the way and doesn't serve any useful purpose, we took the appendix as well," he says. The grin-shaped incision is low on my abdomen. I'm ready for bikini weather.

"How can they yank parts out of you without any written consent?" Christie says, after the doctor leaves. "That would never fly in the US."

Christie is sparkling sun on water. The doctor invites her to sleep over the five days I spend at the Santa Teresa Hospital. "She'll heal a lot quicker with family around," he says.

"That would never be allowed in the US," I say, staring at Christie.

But the doctor is right. My room has a couch bed and with Christie snoring I can feel the incision drawing together in miraculous healing.

I'm homesick and crave news from family. Phone calls cost over two dollars a minute, so mail is the only option. Every day I run to the mail slot, where precious, sacred white envelopes are shoved through to flop onto the ground. But the system is erratic. Sometimes there's nothing for days, then five or six letters arrive together. I learn that my sister won the city-wide Halloween costume contest a month after it happened, that my father had a gall bladder operation six weeks earlier. Verna says that the mailman drinks, that's why delivery is so random. I believe her when I see him staggering to the mail slot with a handful of letters on Christmas day.

I fly home to New Jersey for semester break and convince my dad that I need a car. "You can take Little

Red (a VW Bug with a sunroof)," he says. "I can't go with you this time."

LITTLE RED – FOOTHILLS OF THE APPALACHIANS

Nancy, a girl from the program, helps with driving and in a week we're back in my adopted city. There will be some changes. First, I drop out of the Junior Year Abroad program; at the conservatory I'll live and breathe music and soak up Spanish on the side. Verna will move out to live with Vanesa, another girl in the program.

Everyone loves Little Red. The guys badger me to chauffer them to their girlfriends for balcony serenades on birthdays. It's always after midnight, so I rarely give in. When I do, six or more pile in with instruments, heads sticking out of the sunroof. Police are nowhere.

A car saves me time on public transportation, but I'm a cruising dollar sign for police. They want money for made up offences, like driving too slow in the passing lane, not using a turn signal, even slowing down too soon for a red light.

The government sponsors a trip for the chamber orchestra to perform in Oaxaca State. There, Laura and Carmen, a violist and violinist, invite me to share a room. We spend our days at the pool, surrounded by lush forest. Evenings we perform Brandenburg Concertos and the Marcello Oboe Concerto. I'm back in the royal courts of

LAURA, CARMEN, LAURIE 1976

Austria, jeweled-clad patrons and lavish chandelier receptions. Life doesn't get any better.

Our friendship continues after the tour, even though Laura refuses to talk to Carmen when I spend the night at her house. Unfounded jealousy between girlfriends; a first for me. After a few days of sulking, we're a trio again and spend hours in front of the mirror, trying new makeup and hairdos. They teach me how to use a teaspoon to curl my eyelashes, hand me a Kleenex whenever we go out (no toilet paper anywhere) and explain which boys to avoid ("No! He's from a poor village.") To and from rehearsals and concerts we go, either in Laura's white VW Bug, or in Little Red. With the radio blasting, the wind in our hair, we sing along to Julio Iglesias or Roberto Carlos. We are alive!

I've meshed into Carmen's family now. Her mother calls me *hija postiza,* adopted daughter. Whenever we leave the house, she blesses me, making the sign of the cross on my forehead and chest. I'm not Catholic, but I don't mind. It can't hurt. Carmen's father scolds me as often as he does Carmen for being late for dinner or for wearing too much lipstick. I'm in.

I need to drive to the airport to see if I can convince some stranger going to the States to take a letter to mail there. That way, my family will receive it in a few days. I ask Laura to wait in the car while I run into the airport. I'm gone less than three minutes but, when I return, Little Red is gone. I search the airport parking lots, walk the road around the airport, and then call Carmen. After an hour of circling on foot around the lots, we spot Laura.

"Police stopped me and took the car," she says. "I'm a Mexican, I can't drive a tourist's car. You got me in trouble. On purpose."

"I didn't know," I say.

At the impound lot in Tlalpan, the official wants 3,000 pesos ($240). I don't have it. Carmen calls Leopoldo, the orchestra director and he shows up an hour later. He argues with the police and they return the car for 500 pesos

($40). Laura cuts me off like a gangrenous leg.

Our last tour is to Chihuahua in May. From there I plan
to just keep driving north to New Jersey in Little Red, my
faithful *vochito* (little bug). I kiss my friends good-bye,
thinking it's forever. "Call when you get home," they say.

In the middle of the Chihuahuan Desert, Little Red gets
pneumonia, coughing and losing power. Not a car or
building in sight, she jerks and sputters and dies. I get out
and open the engine hood. A clear liquid drips from a tiny
hole in the fuel pump. Gasoline! It looks like a screw
could fit in the tiny hole, and there, on a two-inch wide
shelf under the leak, the naughty screw sparkles. It fits! I
give it a few turns and try the ignition. The engine sounds
better than new.

I dial up Carmen in Mexico soon after I greet my
parents and siblings with hugs and kisses. Her sister,
Rochis, answers, her voice muffled and strained. "Carmen
and Laura were in a car accident," she says. "Laura is
gone. She's dead," Rochis says it as if even she doesn't
believe it.

Maybe my Spanish is off, I'm not understanding. "Say
it again, slower," I say.

Laura died instantly. Carmen is in intensive care. "It's
better if she doesn't know about Laura," Rochis says.

After the last concert, some of the students went for
dinner. Director Leopoldo followed the girls to make sure
they got home safely. When the traffic light turned green,
Laura pulled onto Avenida Insurgentes without looking.
She never saw the drunk speeding to make the yellow
light, crashing into her door, crushing the life from her.
She was only 18.

After she recovers, Carmen writes five-page letters every week: "The orchestra played for Laura's funeral mass. Everyone came, even Roberto, crying so hard he couldn't hold his cello. Remember? How she always talked about him, but he never asked her out? Now it's too late. The church smelled of white gardenias and incense. We lit red votive candles; the sanctuary was ablaze. I miss you so much. Please come back."

First, I need to get my university degree; it will only take a year. But I'm obsessed with the dream of a passionate, vibrant life I know is waiting for me. Will I ever get back?

1977

RETURN TO PARADISE

Find a job you enjoy doing and you'll never work a day in your life. – Mark Twain

"I'm so proud of you!" my mom says, hugging me at the reception after my final violin recital at college. I gaze at the candlelit table with sandwiches, chocolate cake, and coffee, grateful to all who've come this far with me: my seven brothers and sisters who grudgingly allowed me to use the only bathroom in the house as a practice room; my amazing teacher who scolded me to tears at lessons; and my parents, who, realizing I was not going to "give it up and study for a real job," bought me a violin.

"Why do you have to go to Mexico?" my mom asks. "What's the rush?"

It's the 22nd of May. I've graduated. I'm free. I don't care if anyone misses me. I've waited all year for this. "Just don't fall in love with some Don Juan," she says. "They'll break you." Wisdom I should have packed around my heart. Words I'll always remember.

"I'll be back at the end of the summer," I say, a promise I believe I can keep.

Carmen picks me up at the airport and we drive to her house. Her dad, Don José is packing to fly to Cancun to act in the movie The Bermuda Triangle. I gawk at pictures all over the house of José beaming, his arm draped over the shoulders of Bill Cosby, Rock Hudson, Sammy Davis Jr., Kirk Douglas, Liza Minnelli, John Wayne. He's worked with everyone in Hollywood!

JOSÉ CHAVEZ TROWE, ACTOR EXTRAORDINAIRE

In the last picture, Don José stands between Robert Redford and Paul Newman. "I was the head officer who ordered the ambush of those two," he says, pointing. "When Butch Cassidy and the Sundance Kid played here in Mexico, strangers on the street would stop me. 'You should be ashamed of yourself for what you did,' they'd say." He shakes his head and laughs. "It was a movie!"

That night, Carmen and I whisper until five in the morning. We chat about the accident, how Laura's parents told her never to visit again. Ever. Carmen is a painful reminder of their cherished daughter.

Carmen pulls some strings and that very week we're substituting second violins in a major Mexico City orchestra. They pay me through Carmen because I have a tourist visa and I'm not allowed to work in Mexico. Back only a week and I'm already breaking the law. Truth be told, I would have paid *them to* play with this group.

No sooner are violins and bows packed away at the symphony for the summer, than we're invited to the Mexico State Orchestra.

LAURIE IN THE STATE OF MEXICO SYMPHONY
ORCHESTRA

The first month at our new job, Carmen and I commute the two hours from her parent's house in Mexico City for rehearsal and stay in a hotel Saturday nights after the concert. After one concert, we find three dozen roses in our room. "It's for you, from Fernando," Carmen says, reading the card.

"Isn't he married? With kids?" I say.

"That doesn't matter," Carmen says, handing me the card.

I keep the flowers but look away whenever Fernando smiles at me at rehearsals.

Rafael, a double bassist in the orchestra, is different. One day, he invites us to stay with him. His apartment is impeccable, decorated with colonial-style wood furniture he inherited from his father, including a king-sized bed with a gray, imitation-fur bedspread and an orange-red-yellow shag rug.

In Rafael's bedroom, two items on the bedside table grab my eye: a three-by-five picture of a blue-eyed, three-year-old mini-Rafael, and a pair of earrings. First, I ask about the boy. It's Erik, Rafael's son.

"My ex-wife took him back to Texas a year ago. She won't let me see him, so we don't even talk."

"You don't support him?"

"She'll just spend the money on herself."

"If it makes her feel good, she'll be a better mom."

He shrugs and shakes his head. He doesn't want to talk about it.

Red lights. Now, who owns those earrings?

"They belong to Costanza, a violist in the orchestra," he says.

"Your girlfriend?"

"No, not really."
I've never seen them together.

The commute is exhausting, so Carmen and I look for an apartment in Toluca. I will miss Don Jose and Carmelita who patiently correct my blunders in Spanish and share local wives' tale wisdom. I nod in wide-eyed wonder when they tell me I'll get arthritis from going barefoot on cold, tiled floors, or that I'll die if I cut my hair after eating, or that ingesting cold items (ice cream, jello, soda with ice) when I have a sore throat, will kill me. I don't argue their childlike innocence, but every chance I get, I test for validity and then toss their cautionary tales to the wind.

Carmen and I buy two double beds, a table and chairs, and a kitchen stove and move into an apartment above Rafael. Later that week, Tchaikovsky's Romeo and Juliet blares from below and Rafael yells from his patio, under my balcony. "How about that, my Juliet? Beautiful is it not?" Then, he raises his arms and quotes Orsino's famous lines, "If music be the fruit of love, play on…" I laugh and clap when he bows. I really like this guy.

Heaven is a seat in the violin section of an orchestra. I'm 21 years old living my dream.

At the first rehearsal I meet Enrique Batiz, the director, who not only introduces me to Beethoven's IV Symphony and Rossini's Barber of Seville Overture, but new vocabulary as well: *papucho* (hunk), *maricones and putos* (homosexuals), and *cachondo* (horny).

Another American girl, with 10 years in Mexico, sits across the aisle, in first violins. She doesn't even say hello

22

the first few weeks and then, one day, turns. "Don't stay in Mexico," she says. "Get out while you can." She won't tell me why.

"I love it here and I'm not leaving," I say.

She rolls her eyes and shakes her head. "You'll learn soon. Hope it's not too late."

I don't need to speak Spanish to realize that certain musicians aren't up to the maestro's standards. With a curled-lip stare, he points the baton at the errant trumpet or clarinet and orders them to repeat the same four measures over and over, striking his baton against the podium, faster and faster. Maestro Batiz conducts so fiercely that sweat and saliva spray the string players in the front circle. No one knows what he wants us to do when he stares, in a trance, at the baton circling above his head. We do know, however, the minute the maestro staggers into the hall, if he's had a bad night. Sometimes it looks as if he's come directly from the party. His assistants scurry to guide him up the stairs onto the stage. With bloodshot eyes, the hallmark towel around his neck, he stands behind the podium, glaring, as if we're responsible for his misery. Someone will probably be out of a job by the end of the rehearsal. I'm one of the lucky ones he never picks on.

Queretaro, two hours north of Mexico City, is the first stop on the tour. Carmen and I share one of the bungalows scattered throughout a thick wood. Around 11 PM, a knock on the door. It's Batiz's assistant. The maestro needs to see me in his room. Now.

"Do I have to go?" I ask.

"If you want to keep your job," he says.

We walk in silence through the forest, leaving Carmen farther and farther behind. Arriving at the bungalow, the assistant opens the door and signals for me to enter.

"Come with me!" I say.

He gently pushes me into the room and the door clicks behind me. A single bedside lamp casts the spacious room in a dark yellow shadow. The maestro sits, in the center of a king-sized bed, the covers up to his waist, naked torso.

"How're you doing, Laurita? Are you happy in the orchestra? Come, sit by me," he says, patting the bed next to him.

"I'm fine here." My palms are sweating, my stomach hurts.

"How do you like the tour?"

"I'm learning a lot of repertoire."

"Don't be shy." He pats again.

"I love playing with the guest soloists, especially Maestro Szeryng," I say.

"A fantastic violinist. A national treasure! Come sit!"

"I'm a little dizzy," I say.

"We'll talk later then," he says, waving me away.

The following day, at rehearsal, Batiz's assistant points to a seat at the back of the section. "The maestro says you'll be sitting there from now on," he says, raised eyebrows confirming why I've been demoted.

I don't care where I sit, just as long as it's not in the audience.

I start to notice Rafael. He's loud, always joking, the center of every raucous crowd. One overcast afternoon, I'm sick in bed. My head pounds with a sinus infection. Rafael visits with a bag of oranges. "These will cure you," he says. He has cast his spell, won me over by thoughtfulness. Chemicals flood my brain and I am so blinded and confused, I overlook the fact that he doesn't stay and make the juice. He does say, however, over his shoulder as he opens the door to leave, "You can call me Sonny, all my friends do."

Carmen is jealous that I go back to Sonny's apartment after rehearsals. He teaches me yoga routines and how to meditate, lectures me on spiritual connections with animals and trees. From him I learn about existentialism, Gurdjieff, and Krishnamurti. Sonny is vegetarian, and I discover a hundred ways to prepare black beans and soya. He's a seeker. I've found my soulmate.

On my 22nd birthday, the orchestra travels to San Luis Potosi. The orchestra manager discretely assigns hotel rooms: women in the orchestra bunk with their married lovers, and gay couples are accommodated. Even though we don't live together, we're inseparable, and every stop on this tour Sonny and I receive the same keys to a king-size room.

After the concert, twenty or so of the Americans in the orchestra gather to celebrate my special day at the rotating restaurant on the 10th floor of our hotel. The band is out of tune and limps through old standards, but a tequila haze envelops us and no one cares.

At two in the morning the group packs up but we're just getting started. My friends get their clarinets and trumpets, a few violins and a double bass, and we jam and dance until sunrise. This group of expats sizzles off stage as well as on.

I don't notice when Sonny disappears from the fray; he leaves without a goodbye. At 7 AM, when I return to the room, I find the bed untouched. After a quick shower, I find him roaming the lobby.

"You didn't come to the room last night," I say.

"You and Batiz were dancing plastered together. And you didn't stop him."

"I was dancing with everybody!"

"I thought you were going to spend the night with him!"

"We were all having fun. It was my birthday!"

How do I deal with this? Only time will prove who I am.

In December, Sonny and I are two of six musicians invited to Merida, Yucatan, to coach the orchestra there. They requested teachers who can give a few lessons on trombone, oboe, French horn, bassoon, violin and double bass. The director of the orchestra is content with our work, but the elderly male violinists ignore my suggestions on how to hold their bows or position their violins. I offer exercises to improve vibrato and intonation, but they won't even look at me.

"They're not used to taking orders from a woman," Sonny says, when I complain to him. "This is Macholand."

I'm a woman, I'm young, and I'm American. Three strikes. I'm out.

Our hosts can't pay our salaries, but we're grateful for the plane tickets, the all-you-can-eat buffet, and an austere hotel room Sonny and I share.

LAURIE AND SONNY, CHICHEN ITZA

We're also treated to a visit to the Yucatan's famous pyramids at Chichen Itza. A vibrant energy resonates through us as we walk around the enormous ancient structures. And then, cramps. Sweating and trembling I yell to Sonny, "I need a doctor."

"I've dreamed all my life of this place," he says. "You're not going to ruin it."

"Don't worry. I'll get there on my own."

"I'll take you, Laurie," Don, the trombonist says. "You look awful."

Sonny has a change of heart, as he watches us walk down off the pyramid, and is soon at my side. "I'll take her," he says to Don. A tour guide directs us to a new clinic on the site, recently opened for tourists. I'm assigned to one of three private rooms, a young doctor attaches a saline drip, and I'm out.

"Did you climb to the top of the pyramid?" the nurse asks when I wake. She tells me that the energy that radiates out of the top is powerful and can be dangerous. "Never, ever climb pyramids during menstruation," she says.

This folklore I do believe. I have lived it.

Sonny takes me back to the hotel. All night long the air-conditioner blasts until we're in a freezer, only a thin sheet for warmth. I beg Sonny to raise the temperature. "I'm hot," he says. By the end of the week, coughing bronchitis, I leave for New Jersey.

As time progresses, I realize that, despite his narcissism, I'm infatuated. Sonny is Peter Pan, Mick Jagger, and Don Quixote: care-free, wild, noble. And he's spontaneous: he shows up unexpectedly in New Jersey and convinces me to fly back with him to Never Never Land. We have decided it's time I move in with him.

When the orchestra travels around the state to perform in quaint villages, we never know what kind of venue awaits us. A church, a gymnasium, or even a basketball court is transformed into a concert hall for an evening where poor farmers marvel at Brahms Symphonies and Rococo cello solos. After every concert, the host town always invites us for dinner, tables stocked with tequila, rum and whiskey. We linger until the bottles are empty, then, on the walk to the waiting buses, a few musicians stop at corner stores to buy beer for the ride home. Sonny and I don't care. We push through the lively revelers to the back of the bus, slip into the driver's bed, and draw the curtains.

28

Word leaks that I'm going to the US over winter break, and everyone puts in an order. Even the orchestra bus driver requests a winter jacket. I return with $200 dollars of Pirastro strings and, at the first rehearsal after vacation, bargain-hunting musicians storm me. They're violin vultures on a string feeding frenzy, a flurry of grabbing, promises to pay me later. No one does. When I give the driver his coat, he says, "Later." Forty years and I'm still waiting.

But none of the corruption that whirls around Sonny and me affects our relationship. Not yet. We share exquisite, intimate time together whenever we can, prolonging our waking hours, rushing home to dive into bed after rehearsals, and every night carefully preparing the bedroom with scented candles and fresh sheets for passionate rendezvous. Abundance is everywhere; playing in the orchestra and being with Sonny is more than I ever dreamed possible.

1978

INGRID

The more invisible you try to make me, the more powerful I become. - Anonymous

Sonny sets aside one weekend a month to visit his mother, Ingrid, in Cuernavaca. How can I not love this guy? I know our relationship is serious when he invites me along.

"My mother has never liked any girl I've introduced her to," Sonny says, as we bump along in his powder blue pickup truck. "She's jealous, I guess. Wants all my attention."

Ingrid is elegance. Five pounds of sparkling costume jewelry decorate her neck, wrist and fingers, dyed blond hair in a short perm. Dressed in tight jeans and a billowy chiffon red and yellow shirt, Ingrid looks young for her 65 years. She's had surgery for cataracts and the velvet black pupils spill into her sky-blue irises. I kiss her cheek and shake hands. She reeks of Channel #5 and cigarettes. I'm in jeans, a simple peasant shirt and sandals. No make-up. She looks me over, rolls her eyes, and turns to Sonny. I've disappeared.

She leads us to the dining table set with white linen tablecloth and napkins, cut glass crystal and green transparent dishes. She's prepared a home-cooked meal of goulash, steamed asparagus tips and Waldorf salad. Sonny's favorite.

After lunch, Ingrid hands Sonny a list of odd jobs she wants done around the house, and then retires to her room where, sprawled on her bed, she watches Mexican soap operas, sips ice-loaded Cokes, and chain smokes all afternoon. Sometimes three cigarettes burn at once: one in the kitchen ashtray, one in the bedroom ashtray, and the one she's just lighting.

Ingrid knows that Sonny and I are crazy in love, but she's adamant about assigning us separate bedrooms. "You'll offend the maid if she sees you sleeping together. Everyone knows you aren't married!" she says.

Sonny shrugs. He's tender and attentive to her every whim. I can expect the same.

Over time, I become a regular visitor and Ingrid politely tolerates me. Occasionally, we breeze in on Bridge day. Ingrid covers the round table with a green felt tablecloth, sets out bowls of peanuts and ashtrays, and fires up a pot of coffee.

Three elderly ladies arrive, bleached hair teased into giant puffballs, Maraschino-cherry lips and buffed French nails. Chunky jewelry hangs from their wrists and necks like gaudy Christmas tree ornaments, and a scent of Marlboro Lights trails them. For the next three hours, lively chatter and laughter spill from the room, where the ladies are not to be disturbed.

Ingrid and friends start a nonprofit organization called Amigos de la Música (Friends of Music), and they host concerts by Sonny's chamber orchestra, Camerata Mexicana, in elegant private homes. Ingrid does it for one reason: to lure Sonny to town.

I'm red-eyed tired, but Sonny convinces me to attend the first concert of the series. Ingrid is seated behind a table taking tickets at the door and waves me in.

The next day, Ingrid invites us for lunch. As soon as the dishes are cleared, Sonny leaves to wash Ingrid's car. We're alone at the table. She lights up a cigarette and blows smoke above my head, following the trail with her eyes. "Yesterday I was too ashamed to introduce you to my friends," she says. She takes another drag and then continues. "You looked so pale and washed-out. If you don't start fixing yourself up with some makeup and jewelry, Sonny is going to find somebody else who cares about how they look."

Wearing makeup in my house was forbidden. "You look like whores, you're not leaving the house like that," my dad would say, if he caught us with colored lips or painted nails. Mascara or rouge was as bad for our souls as cigarettes for our lungs.

"You don't give your son much credit," I say, instead. "He's not that shallow."

"I know men," she says, lighting another cigarette. "You're going to lose him."

On the way home, staring at the dotted white line pulsing from the darkness, I tell Sonny about Ingrid's prediction.

"I told you, my mom doesn't like any girl that I bring home," Sonny says. "Don't worry. She'll get used to having you around soon enough."

I sigh. Ingrid is a German-Danish immigrant. She speaks five languages, once owned a classy night-club, and was married five times, twice to Sonny's dad. She was a trailblazer. If I weren't dating her son, we'd probably be friends and she'd most likely invite me to join the ladies at the Bridge table.

1979

A GIFT

*In the sea there are countless treasures, but if you desire
safety, it is on the shore. - Saadi*

Month after month a spot of blood triggers a day of
mourning: I light votive candles on bedside and kitchen
tables and along the bathroom sink, then spend the day in
bed with a box of tissues. My doctor says I'll never have
kids because of the wedges he took from my ovaries.
There's nothing I want more.

"You're so dramatic," Sonny says. He makes me
soothing teas and rubs my feet, then shuts himself in the
spare bedroom to practice.

In department stores I caress miniature booties, turning
away when smiling clerks ask my due date, I visit Phyllis
and rock her baby Rachel until my arms ache, and I buy
What to Name Your Baby, hoping that if I get the name
right, I'll get the prize.

Finally, after a year of failures, I miss a period, and
then another. One day, alone at home, I yell upstairs to

Carmen and ask her to accompany me to the nearest pay phone. "I had tests done and I need the results."

The receiver crackles, and then, the receptionist's words, like a voice from heaven, "It's positive."

Did I hear right? "Does that mean I'm pregnant?" I hold my breath.

"You are," she says. "If you're not happy, we can counsel you about other options." I slam down the phone and burst from the red phone booth into Carmen's arms. We dance in circles down the sidewalk.

I'm on a sacred mission: I decline invitations to parties, buy out bookstores of anything with a baby on the cover, and refuse to take even aspirin or nose drops.

Sonny just nods his head when I tell him. He knows how much I've wanted this. But, a couple of years ago his ex-wife took their three-year-old baby and returned to Texas. He hasn't seen them since. "I can see it happening all over again," he says. So, he continues his bachelor lifestyle and, when I'm almost ready to deliver, decides to accompany Marcos on a mystical-mushroom cave experience.

We agree that I'll fetch them in Sonny's pick-up truck the next day. I arrive at noon, the designated time, and while I wait, an old shepherd with a 30-head flock wanders by.

"Have you seen two men around here?" I ask. "They went in yesterday."

"People disappear all the time," he says, eyeing the mouth of the cave. "It's a maze of tunnels. You make the wrong turn and you're gone forever." He waves away a cloud of dust and follows the sheep as they nibble their way up into the hills.

After two hours of sweating in noonday heat, my voice hoarse from shouting into the musty darkness, I decide to go for help. It's a ten-minute drive to town and as I turn down the main street, I see them sitting on a curb, drinking beer and laughing.

"We got hungry, so we just walked back," Sonny beams.

I want to strangle the life out of him, but I'll need his help changing diapers. Little do I know.

I thought that nature knew best and the baby would arrive when he was ready. Three weeks late, I call the doctor. "Is it a boy or girl?" he asks, assuming I already have my treasure.

"No, nothing, yet," I say.

"This is dangerous," he says, and schedules a cesarean for the next day. At midnight, burning pain wakes me.

Sonny drives me to the Santa Teresa Hospital, and we park across the street. I need to walk the rest of the way but halfway across the road pain squeezes the breath from me. I freeze. Water gushes from between my legs.

"You can't just stop in the middle of the road," Sonny says, shaking his head. "You're holding up traffic."

"I can't move!" I moan.

A car door opens. "Can I help?" a man's voice yells.

"She'll be fine," Sonny says, waving him away.

I want a natural birth but, after 10 hours of sea-sick nausea and what feels like a molten-hot butcher knife shoved into my vagina every two minutes, I'm exhausted and the medics are pacing. Without asking, they flop me on my side and jam a three-inch needle between my vertebrae. I can't feel my legs. Minutes later I'm wheeled away.

"Push!" voices yell in the delivery room. That's impossible. Half my body is dead. A white gown climbs onto my bed and two hands pump on my upper belly. Five more minutes and the baby flops out into waiting hands.

"Here's your boy," white gown says, plopping him on my chest. I sob and slobber kisses. And then, still counting fingers, he's whisked away. All day I beg for my baby. An eternity later, a young nurse arrives swinging him from side-to-side face down the length of one forearm. She hands me a life. And leaves.

He's as wrinkled and red as a dehydrated mango sprinkled with chili powder. "That's what happens when you're in the water too long," I whisper. A few strands of hair stand gel-erect the length of his head. "That's why you took so long, they were spiffing you up to meet me," I say. He flutters his eyelids, wrinkles his nose and cries, experimenting with sound. My universe is whole, this is ecstasy.

Sonny decides to name our baby Pedro (Peter), after Ingrid's Danish father. Maybe that way she'll accept her new grandson. Sonny didn't even tell her we were expecting.

Petey begins every night in his Moses-style wicker basket next to our bed. Barely a whimper and I'm up, trembling excited, breathing in the damp sour smell of his newborn head. Wedging him into the warm space between Sonny and me I nurse and change him. The bedside lamp glares, Petey hums, and Sonny snores.

I'm lucky that the orchestra gives me three months paid leave to stay home and learn how to be a mom. My sisters in the US don't get this luxury. But the three months fly by and too soon orchestra rehearsals call. I can't leave my bundle. He's vulnerable, no nanny in the world will do. Sonny helps me find twenty-year-old Bernarda, recommended by the orchestra manager. "It will be fine," Sonny says. "I had a nanny until I was 13 years old."

Bernarda adores Petey. He claps when he sees her and they sing and play the hours away. Still, three-hour rehearsals are torture. I obsess about Petey.

One day, at rehearsal, my stand partner Jorge says "Your blouse is wet."

I look down to see two silver dollar-size wet circles. Fellow musicians are like family and he's trying to help. But I want to disappear. I pack up and slip out early.

Petey is six months old when the manager announces a two-week tour. We'll play concerts for the workers of the state-run gas monopoly and their families at the nine oil ports along the Gulf of Mexico. I'm not leaving my baby behind.

Only half the orchestra fits in the WWII twin engine DC6 planes, so for each section of the journey, the plane makes two trips. There are no seats, and we bounce around on the floor like loose marbles, Petey vomiting my milk on every flight.

At one concert, I find a little room backstage and, on top of a mountain of dusty maroon curtains, I lay out a blanket for Petey. Even though the boys who set up the stands and chairs agree to watch him, I hold my breath at every pause in the music during the concert. What if he screams? At intermission I race backstage and find Petey's nursery is now the maestro's dressing room. Soon, it's buzzing with well-wishers but no one notices Petey, still asleep in the corner.

Everywhere strangers pet my baby and offer advice: Don't sit him up too soon or the soft spot on his head will sink; don't force him to walk or he'll be bowlegged; pile blankets on him even in summer because he's used to the heat of your womb. I toss all that advice like a wrinkled program after a concert. But there is one old wives' tale I heed, mainly because it's convenient: nursing a baby is a reliable contraceptive. But five months after Petey's birth, nursing full time, I'm pregnant again. We busted that myth. Sonny murmurs something about babies getting all the attention. I grab him and twirl.

1980

LITTLE CABIN IN THE WOODS

You will never be completely at home again because part of your heart will always be elsewhere. That is the price you pay for the richness of loving and knowing people in more than one place. - Mirian Adeney

Eight years of faithful service, and Maestro Batiz still won't consider Sonny for principal of the bass section; he hires only foreigners for that position. Tired of waiting for a change in policy, Sonny auditions and aces first chair for an orchestra in Mexico City.

Petey is almost a year old and we're expecting a new baby in a few months. I refuse to raise my kids in the air polluted cacophony of Mexico City. Sonny's mom lives in Cuernavaca, The City of Eternal Spring, a logical place to look for a home.

At the same time, we learn that Ivan, Sonny's boyhood friend, crashed his motorcycle head-on into a tree to avoid hitting a dog, and died. The grieving family is eager to sell Ivan's dream: the shell of a one-room, cinder-block cabin in Huitzilac.

It's cozy. To the left is a living-room with a floor-to-ceiling volcanic-stone fireplace. To the right, string-wrapped stakes in the dirt floor map out a kitchen and bathroom. A loft sits above the living room and the roof is made of corrugated asbestos. It's nestled in 10,000 meters of crispy-cool, pine-scented forest at the end of a dirt road. Wild innocence. Sonny will have a 45-minute drive to his new job in Mexico City. Perfect. We find a three-bedroom house in Cuernavaca to rent while we finish our dream house.

1980

AN OMEN

As for omens, there is no such thing as an omen. Destiny does not send us heralds. She is too wise or too cruel for that. - Oscar Wilde

I step out of the car into my emerald temple, earthy pine incense, angels murmuring through swaying boughs, our two-acre paradise. I love it here, dreaming of the day the cabin will be finished and spring to life with colorful piñatas, squawking chickens, stargazing and bonfires. My baby jumps and I rub my six-month belly. She's never done this before. A sense of uneasiness washes over me.

This place is finally ours, we have a healthy one-year-old with another on the way, and playing in the orchestra with Sonny is a dream come true. Why this sense of foreboding? Soon, my worries are put to rest.

"Look Sonny," I say, holding up a dirty, high-top baby boot I find in the weeds. "The locals say finding a shoe means good luck."

"We already have all the luck we need," he says. "We

have everything!"

Sonny embraces life with exuberant passion whatever the occasion.

Dark clouds rumble; a storm is moving in. We need to go. Ten minutes up the road, we stop in Huitzilac at a mom-and-pop corner store. The town bustles with the annual fair honoring Saint John the Baptist. Barking dogs chase a family of pigs; a pair of lazy horses amble by; a handful of young boys, hoping to win a stuffed bear, aim darts at balloons; a carousel blasts lively calliope tunes; and greasy onion and beef smoke billows from taco stands. This quaint *pueblito* is an hour south of Mexico City, but we just traveled a hundred years back in time. Chips and juice in hand, we continue our journey.

No shoulder now, we wind through pine-tree tunnels, mountains on the left, a drop-off to the right. Feeling nauseous, I recline the seat and close my eyes.

Just past the Zempoala Lagoons, Sonny stares at the rear-view mirror and whispers, "Oh-oh." Simple as that. Not even a real word to warn me. I turn and look past Sonny.

A white car is passing, four guns aimed at our heads. They cut us off. Stop. Out jump three armed sombreros, red handkerchiefs hiding faces. One yanks Sonny out, shoves him in the back seat, gun to his head, another replaces Sonny as the driver, and the last jumps in the front passenger seat, shoving me to the middle over the hand brake.

"Don't hurt her," Sonny says. "She's pregnant."

Oh God, Sonny. Don´t make them angry. "We know," the man in the back says, striking Sonny in the head with his gun. "Look away."

Mile after mile we follow the ambush car. I'm wheezing, can't breathe. Are they going to kill us?

For weeks we'd planned this day, attention to every detail so it would be perfect. We left Petey with Carmen, my baby-loving best friend. Why drag our one-year-old on a four-hour trip, just to bounce around in a hot car?

"We'll close on the house, deposit to the roofer to buy the beams and tiles, and be back in time for dinner," Sonny had said. "Petey won't even notice we're gone."

A cashier's check would protect us from bandidos looking to take our nest egg. But when Sonny redeemed the check in Cuernavaca, the teller gave him 150,000 pesos (6,000 USD) in 1,000-peso bills. He counted one hundred and fifty bills with an audience of impatient tellers and patrons. Then, they all watched as he shoved the roll into the front pocket of his jeans.

As we trekked through downtown bustle to the realtor's office, I was on alert, glancing behind for anyone trailing us. Everyone seemed to be about their own business.

Contract signed without incident, we hustled on to the roofer's, but the office was deserted-dark and the phone dead.

"Petey's never been without me overnight," I'd said. "It's five o'clock. Let's go."

"We need to pay for the roof. I need to get rid of this load of cash."

An hour later, the sun low on the horizon and no chance of unloading our stash, we headed for home. "Let's check out our land," Sonny had said. "It's on the way."

And so, we stopped, and my baby hurtled against me, and I found the shoe. And now this. Oh God.

I'm suffocating, sobbing, my belly is hard; the men on either side shove their guns between their legs. They're hiding their weapons. My body shudders. Pain sucks my breath away. Will my baby live if she comes now? My mind won't stop.

Finally, a half hour later, we turn onto a dirt road. Please no! Lush forest swallows us. Oh God, no one to save us. No one to know our death. I lean my arms and head on the dashboard. More contractions. Rapid shallow breathing. A mile more and we stop. The sky is tarnished silver; thunder threatening rain. Will we be alive to feel it?

The men drag Sonny into the trees, leaving me in the car with the driver, not more than 15 years old. He drums his fingers on the steering wheel. I wait for the gunshot. "Did you see us at the bank?" I ask, trying to hijack any thoughts he might have of harming me. A sharp pain, and I double over.

"No," he says, staring outside. "Not there."

Silence. Even the birds are still; the world has died around us.

The bandidos are back. Without Sonny.

"Get out!" It's raining, a light sprinkle, like a holy water blessing. I ask if I can get my jacket from the backseat. "Yes," the ringleader barks. And then to the men: "Nobody touches her." Despite the boss's orders, the punk driver yanks off my wristwatch. He pulls a rope from his back pocket and ties it around my wrist, then drags me to a tree.

"They've seen us!" the boss yells, just in time to distract the boy from my other wrist. "Let's get out of here!"

But there's no one.

Frozen, I gaze as our brand-new Volkswagen Rabbit disappears into the verdant blur. They'll find my purse with spare change and pictures of Petey that I hid under the seat.

Shouting. Someone's calling. My belly tightens, pain, I drop to my hands and knees panting. The rain falls in full drops, slow-motion soothing. "I'm over here," Sonny yells.

A twenty-yard hobble through blackberry prickers and I find him standing, hands bound behind a giant oak. "You should've seen their eyes light up when they pulled out that roll of bills," he says, as I untie him. "Look, they didn't find this in my other pocket. We've got 150 pesos." He's born-again euphoric and hugs me. I sob into his neck.

Contractions stop, the baby is still.

"We've survived one crisis together and you're not even born yet," I say as I rub my belly.

It's pouring now and we're drenched, convulsive shivering. Out on the highway, we signal the first car, but the driver speeds by. Sonny jumps to the center white line, waving his arms, rope dangling from his wrist.

"Today's not my day to die!" he shouts at the sky. A red pick-up truck stops.

"We were just robbed!" Sonny says into the driver's window, dangling the rope from his wrist.

"They're always holding people up out here," the driver says, lowering the glass. "It's the locals taking advantage. Police are in on it too."

We hop into the cab and head back to the town we just left.

"So much for those baby shoes being a good omen," I say, untying the rope.

"They just wanted the money," Sonny says. "They didn't kill us. I'd say those shoes were spot on."

1980

ANOTHER BLOW

What is the lesson I haven't learned? - Me

After the kidnapping I tell Sonny to ask for our deposit on the land back. "It's a bad omen," I tell him. "I'm afraid to live there now." But the owners refuse; there's no turning back.

Two weeks after the kidnapping, Sonny convinces me to drive out to see the cabin. "It won't be so bad," he says. "We'll fix it up and it'll be a nice place for the kids to grow up."

We've had visitors. The hardwood floor and beams of the loft are gone. The asbestos roof has vanished. Every pane of glass in the cheap, iron framed windows is broken, our dream shattered.

The sun casts shadows across the dirt floor as it moves across the roof support beams. "They ran out of time and left the structure," Sonny says, gazing at blue sky where a roof used to be. I shake my head, choked by the lump in my throat. I hug Sonny and sob into his chest. Petey tugs at my pants.

First, the kidnapping, now this. I don't want to bring my kids up in this mean-spirited place, but I have no choice. I need to make the best of this: pick up the pieces of our broken dream and piece it back together the best way I know how.

CASSANDRA AND PETEY, ROOF AND LOFT GONE

1980

A TREASURE

No one in human history ever loved anyone as much as I love you. - Me to my kids

I want to be settled in our cozy cabin when the new baby arrives, but the robberies have set us back and we're still in the Cuernavaca rental when the due date approaches. I check the calendar on the kitchen wall. My second baby isn't due for another two weeks, but I'm bleeding.

Sonny and his friend Marcos sprawl in the overstuffed red chairs in the living room.

"The baby might come today," I say, gathering scattered wooden blocks.

"Can we finish our beer first?" Sonny laughs.

"Marcos isn't coming with us, and you can stop drinking now."

"Cheers! To the new baby!" Marcos says, lifting his beer.

I realize that I love and hate Sonny for the same reason: he's laid back and fun-loving. That was fine when we were single, but we have two little lives to think about now. I feel like Wendy caring for the Lost Boys, still pretending at life. Do I need to lighten up?

All day people drift in and out. At noon, Arturo and Gabriela, friends from the conservatory, arrive unannounced with their two toddlers. I shove enchiladas in the oven, throw ice in the lemonade and then lock myself in the bathroom to count the minutes between contractions on my Timex. Just as I finish washing the dishes, Cherie and Jorge, an oboist and violist from the orchestra, surprise us. I might as well enjoy the company for the evening; it'll probably take my body another 12 hours to get ready for the grand finale.

Just past midnight pain jolts me awake, contractions every ten minutes. I wake Sonny.

"The car only has a quarter of a tank," he says sitting up.

"I warned you this morning," I say. "Go get gas."

While he's gone, I shove a tiny white T shirt and some diapers into a backpack, then put a load of Petey's clothes in the roller washing machine. After sweeping and mopping the kitchen, I crank the rollers, running circles every time pain grips me.

I shake snoring Marcos and whisper for him to move to my bed where Petey sleeps. Can he watch him until we return?

From the second story window I pause and watch the world sleep, a streetlight casting eerie shadows through the mist. We'll receive another gift tonight. I think. Are we worthy?

Sonny is finally back, his mother Ingrid emerging from the passenger side, a cup of black coffee in one hand and a lit cigarette in the other. "I couldn't sleep so I took a sleeping pill, and now this," she says. "Mexico City is two hours away. You want your baby born on the side of the road? I called the local hospital, and a doctor is waiting."

My cheeks burn. I look down and blink back angry tears, ashamed that he's dragged his mother into this.

As we break free from zigzagging back alleys and soar over railroad tracks, a ten-foot orange moon greets us from the horizon. Mother and son chat like long lost comrades, while I twist and turn in a watery dream on the back seat. The warm, humid night buzzing with cricket song comforts me. I hope the birth is quick; I don't want to disappoint Ingrid.

"I'm calling an anesthesiologist," the doctor says when we arrive.

"No, I want a natural birth."

"Why would you want to suffer, if you don't have to?" Ingrid says.

I lock myself in the bathroom and the doctor bangs on the door: "Come out this instant! The anesthesiologist is waiting."

When the pounding stops, I crack open the door. A man in a white coat and face mask is measuring liquid into a baby-bottle-size syringe he holds in the air. Two blue gowns and caps lead me to a table and tell me to lie on my side. A surge of water and I feel a tiny head.

"It's here," I yell.

"You can't have a baby on this table!" says chubby blue-gown. "We've got to move her!"

My body is possessed, trembling and pushing, out of my control. No time to move now.

Minutes later, a bluish-yellow blur flutters out from between my legs and then everyone scatters to the far side of the room with the baby. No crying, no shouting. Silence. They don't want to tell me. Minutes pass. An eternity. "Is it dead?" I ask.

"No. You have a *mujercita*," a little woman.

"Why doesn't she cry?"

Why don't they tell me? Will she live?

"The cord was wrapped around her neck. You'll hear her scream any minute."

I'm torn and need stitches. The anesthesiologist finally gets his turn, injecting a yellow liquid into the saline drip and then jabbing a needle between my legs.

Six stitches later I'm in the recovery room, wondering what Sonny and Ingrid are doing, if they've seen the baby. Blood is pooling under my bed and two nurses lift the green sheet. "She's hemorrhaging, could bleed to death," one whispers to the other, as if I'm unconscious. My life-force seeping away, the doctor returns, inserts another mystery liquid into my veins and I drift away.

My baby weighs only 2.07 kilos (4 lbs. 2 oz.), so she's isolated in an incubator "for observation." I ache to hold her, to tell her how sorry I am that she's so tiny, sorry that after the kidnapping I stopped eating, sorry that I dragged her into this suffering.

Alone in a private room with bath, I ring the buzzer. No one answers, so I slip from my bed and begin the five-step trek on my own, pushing the saline drip stand, the needle tugging at my arm. Almost there, the room darkens. I blindly retrace a blood trail and faint into the bed. A nurse rouses me: "What a mess! You had no business getting up."

Ignoring the scolding, I ask her if she's checked my baby's blood type. "If she's RH positive, then I'm going to need an injection."

"I know," she snaps. They haven't done the test.

In an hour she's back with a bedpan and the results: "She's negative," she says.

Sonny arrives with fruit and flowers. "She's wrinkled red," he says.

I want to name her Roxanne, in honor of my sister, but will need to ask my dad first.

The following day, Sonny sends his mom to take us home. He has to work. The orchestra would give him the day off. Why doesn't he take it? Is he overwhelmed by the idea of taking care of two babies?

Back at home a surprise awaits: Bernarda, Petey's nanny in Toluca, arrived yesterday unexpectedly! She traveled over four hours just to visit Petey and agrees to stay for a month to care for him.

The stitches are infected, and I prop a reading lamp between my legs, the heat soothing. The doctor recommends penicillin but after a day I'm full of giant mosquito-shaped bumps and my throat is swelling. I'm allergic to penicillin.

Eight months later my younger sister, Clara, visits. She shares all the news from home, tends to the kids, and answers the phone the day the lawyer for the OSEM calls.

"When are you coming back to the orchestra?" he asks. "It would make my job of getting you working papers a lot easier if you and Sonny would just get married."

"I don't know how serious our relationship is," Sonny says when I tell him about the lawyer's call. "Marriage changes people. You'll probably leave me and take the kids."

"It's two-kids serious," I say. "And I'm taking the kids

on vacation to New Jersey on Monday, wedding or no wedding."

Sonny finally agrees to the lawyer's suggestion to sign the legal documents and we scramble to find witnesses. David and Norma Clay, the couple I lived with the year I studied at the Conservatory, agree to come. From my closet I dig out a folkloric, below-the-knee, purple dress and on Friday, the 13th of June, we drive to the Justice of the Peace while Clara babysits at home.

The judge gives an inspiring speech: "You have two children and you still want to get married! Amazing. I foresee a long happy union."

On the way back to the house David and Norma buy a bucket of Kentucky Fried Chicken. I hate KFC. An emptiness overwhelms me, so I feign a headache and slip into bed, Sonny's laughter filling the house.

1981

KARMA

Imagine the world if everyone lived as you. - My mom's interpretation of I. Kant theory

Tending to a newborn and a one-year-old leaves me bone-tired at the close of every day, so I'm thrilled when Sonny and Sergio, a cellist in the orchestra, bring Patty home.

"She's my girl," Sergio says, gazing into her eyes. "Her parents kicked her out because she's dating me. They know I'm married."

I give Sonny my best you've-got-to-be-kidding glare.

"She can cook and clean in exchange for room and board," he says. "It's a win-win."

I'm uneasy about letting a stranger into my house, especially a homewrecker. She's not getting anywhere near our kids.

Patty, 18 years old, washes clothes by hand, disinfects floors and bathrooms and cooks up delicious enchiladas. After the kids are asleep, she brushes my hair while we watch My Little Angel, my favorite *telenovela*, soap opera.

56

One evening Patty goes out and by midnight I'm worried. I peek into her room to see if she's taken her things. In the corner I see my black chiffon concert gown overflowing from a market bag. My cheeks burn, my heart races. Underneath lie my lacy underwear and designer jeans. I drop to the bed. What did you expect? She steals husbands, this is petty cash.

On her return she sees I've taken back my things, realizes her theft has been discovered. "What were you doing in my room?" Patty says.

"When you didn't come home, I was worried," I say. "We trusted you."

"You can't accuse me of stealing. I didn't take anything from your house."

For the next three years Sergio ignores me backstage at the orchestra. Sonny says not to worry. "He'll come around." Then, one day Sergio stops me in the hall: "I can't believe you kicked Patty out," he says, alcohol on his breath. "She was helping you. You could've spared a few of your things." He shakes his head and bites his lip. "But then, she was stupid to get caught."

1981

THE WEDDING BAND

Only trust someone you would share a bed with, and even then, it's risky. - Judith Gonzalez

A couple of scrawny, unshaven men say they've come to retile my walk-in bathroom closet. I'm alone in the house with my two babies, so I call Sonny.

"Did you schedule this? Should I worry about my clothes and jewelry?"

"The owners of the house sent them over so they must be trustworthy," Sonny says.

That evening, I accompany them to the main gate, eyeing their cloth knapsacks for any unusual bulges. One man points to Pete´s Tyke Bike, "That needs a new seat. I know someone who can fix it."

"Can you take it and drop it off?" I ask. "And let me know when it's ready?"

After a month of excuses and no bike, I ask for the repair shop's address. "I´m going to pick it up, ready or not."

"The truth is," he says, eyeing the second story bathroom window, "someone stole it from the shop."

The day he brings his wife to mix cement, I hover outside the closed bathroom door, muffled voices warning me of imminent evil. I don't want to accuse or offend, so I say nothing.

Finally, the last iridescent blue mosaic tapped into place, we say goodbye. I sigh and shake my head. I finally have my privacy back.

But a few weeks later the trio is back, this time to trim the bougainvillea. Baby Roxy squirms in one arm and two-year-old Petey tugs the other. "This is a bad time," I say.

My gaze wanders to the woman's hand. Is that my custom-made wedding ring? She knows I've seen it and heads for the back of the house. Do I follow her or watch the Tyke-bike thieves? Roxy whimpers, Petey pulls on my dress.

The woman is back. My sacred band gone from her calloused hand.

"Where is the ring you were wearing?" I say.

"That was just an old piece of paper. I tossed it."

"Where? Where is it?"

"I don't know," she says, pretending to scan the bushes.

"Hand it over or I'm calling the police." To hell with civility.

The kids freeze.

She digs it from her purse and slaps it in my hand.

"Call the police if it's yours," I say, fearing I might be wrongfully accusing the woman. "Go ahead. Use my phone."

She turns and stomps to the end of the block, then

stares back. She's crying.

"Is this her ring?" I ask her husband.

"You recognize your own things, don't you?" he says.

"You need to leave," I say. It's rude, but I don't care.

That evening, when Sonny gets home, I tell him what happened. "What am I not getting?" I say. "Why do I keep getting this same lesson over and over? Am I supposed to stop trusting people?"

"It's not about that at all," Sonny says. "It's about freeing yourself of attachments."

1981

THE MOVE

Commitment means staying loyal to what you said you were going to do long after the mood you said it in has left you. - Orebela Gbenga

Symphony concerts, jeweled gowns and champagne receptions, my former life, has vanished. Now, the highlights of my day are the squeaking motorcycle brakes announcing the mailman's delivery of month-old news from my sister; visits from the handsome, curly-headed teenagers who ladle fresh milk from metal cans out of the back of a rusty pickup truck, and rocking my babies to sleep as the soap opera, Angelita, flickers with the drama of a preteen socialite and her family. Isolated, alone, time ticks, second-by-second.

A cactus-bordered highway north calls, but love confuses the matter, and I stay.

It takes a year to rebuild our vandalized house and finally, it's moving day. We borrow a pick-up truck and neighbors show up to load. Even the piano fits. Sonny and Robert head up the hill, singing and smoking, flicking ash and cigarette butts out the window. Pete, Roxy and I follow behind in our VW Beetle. It's dark when we arrive, but we need to set up the beds. With my right hand I hold the kids, one at a time, on my shoulder, and start up the perpendicular ladder, nailed to the edge of the loft. I need to let go with my left hand to reach for the next rung. I can't miss, or we'll both plummet backwards to the floor below.

The king-size bed assembled, I snuggle in between Pete and Roxy and fall asleep reading to them. An hour later, I awake enveloped in a cloud of smoke. "You guys smoking a lot down there?" I say.

It's thick now, the kids are coughing. We check the

fireplace and the stove, then I notice a tendril of smoke seeping from a mattress leaning against the wall. I look behind and flame leaps to my sleeve. Sonny knocks me to the floor and smothers me in curtains, then throws water on the mattress. "Caught it just in time," he says.

The next day, I find a cigarette butt inside the mattress.

1982

GRANDMA INGRID

Narcissistic sons are the revenge of the mother-in-law.
- Me

It's a nightmare to visit Ingrid with toddlers. Her three Great Danes, towering over my babies, drip toilet-water (their drinking bowl) saliva on their hands and faces. I beg Ingrid to shut the dogs in a room just for the hour we visit, but the answer is always the same: "That would be cruel."

Then, an incident that ends our visits forever.

After lunch, unaware that one of the monster dogs is underneath the table chewing a bone, I set one-year-old Roxy down to explore. A minute later, barking, shrieks, and I drag Roxy out, blood pouring from a bite on her forehead. I gather her up and run to the car as Ingrid explains. "He was protecting his food," she says. "We can't blame him for that!"

If private homes are a nightmarish hell, restaurants are a flaming inferno, but that's where Ingrid choses to celebrate Sonny's birthday. After ordering, I try to interest the kids in Matchbox cars and superhero coloring books I pull from my 20-pound rainbow-splashed diaper bag. They throw the crayons on the floor and run the cars off the table.

"Let's explore!" Petey says, grabbing Roxy's hand. I follow as they wind through the tables, stopping to ask other diners what's on their plates, pulling silverware off tables, and then wandering into the kitchen, a bubbling, sizzling toddler's house of horrors. When we finally loop around to our table, Ingrid is paying the bill. Does anyone care that I am starving? The waiter hands me a doggie bag and rolls his eyes as the kids dig into pockets on his apron.

It's Christmas, Pete is three and Roxy two, and I am flying to New Jersey to visit my family. Ingrid says that instead of spending money on trips, we should add a new bathroom onto the house, or hire a full-time gardener. I'm starved for adult conversation; I miss my sisters. This money is well spent.

But my trip gets off to a bad start at the airport ticket counter.

"The travel agent who sold me the ticket said that my baby can travel for free," I say, jiggling Roxy in my arms.

"She can travel on your lap until the age of two," he says. "You need to buy her a ticket."

"Please," I beg. "I have no cash and I can't leave without her!"

"You need to buy a ticket," he says. "Now step aside. Next!"

"Sonny, what do I do?" I say. "I can't go."

"Go! And have a good time," Sonny says. "I'll watch Roxy."

Petey claps and sings on the seat next to me. "Don't cry Mummy," he says.

When I open the suitcase, Roxy's frilly dresses spill out onto the floor. I hug myself and rock. Three weeks drag by and finally we're jetting back.

Sonny and Roxy meet us at the airport and, when I stoop to lift her, Roxy pushes me away. I suggest she stay with me while Sonny fetches the car, but she clings to his leg. I'm melting. Soon, Pete, Roxy and I are in the back seat and, as he drives, Sonny says:

"When the orchestra started up again after vacation, I had to leave Roxy with my mom. She made her lunch every day and locked the dogs in the bedroom. She adores her."

1982

ROXY'S POISON

Whoever destroys a single life is as guilty as though he had destroyed the entire world; and whoever rescues a single life earns as much merit as though he had rescued the entire world. – The Talmud.

I sit on a towel in the yard, the midday sun brilliant, Petey and Roxy five feet away, exploring the inside of the tent where my sister and her boyfriend are staying.

"Mummy, Roxy's taking medicine," Petey says, in tattle-tale cadence.

Rushing into the tent I find two-year-old Roxy, mouth full of pills, tight little fists clutching a bottle of the tranquilizer Valium 4. I jam my finger into her mouth, scooping out little bits and then gather her up. My mind races: No phone. No car. What do I do?

"Roxy needs a hospital!" I yell to the four roofers, as I run by. "Please, watch Petey."

"I'll go with you," Jorge, the foreman, says.

He jumps down from the roof and we rush out to the

main road, 200 yards down a dirt road. I stick out my thumb. Two little grandmas stop, and we jump in the back with Roxy. She's fading. It's taking too long. No one says a word. I think we're lost but then, the hospital. I race with my precious bundle, past the sign-in desk, down the long hall, and through the NO ADMITTANCE-AUTHORIZED PERSONNEL ONLY double doors. Between gasps I blurt out my crisis to a stethoscope draped doctor, a clipboard in hand. "We'll take care of her," a flutter of white coats says. I´m dragged out to the waiting room, a thin partition-wall away.

My roofer companion, Jorge waits in an orange plastic chair. Roxy is screaming and sobbing, I drop next to him.

"Everything's going to be fine," Jorge says, without lifting his head.

Roxy's cries continue, "*Mamá, mamá.*" I wipe my eyes and rush back in. She's on a metal table, arms and legs bound to her body with a tightly wound white sheet. A thin transparent rubber tube hangs from her tiny nose and a nurse holds a small rubber suction ball on the end.

"I'm staying!" I say, and wrap my arms around her trembling body, kissing her forehead and whispering, "I love you." She whimpers. I try to keep her awake.

"Look!" the nurse says, pointing to the rubber tube as she pumps water in and then sucks it out. "You can see the little chewed up pieces coming out! Just in time. We're lucky."

Tears, whispers of gratitude.

My Roxy is saved.

That night, when my sister's boyfriend arrives, I meet him at the gate.

"We almost lost Roxy because you guys left your

Valium lying around."

"What were your kids doing in our tent? They had no business in there," he says.

But there are good people everywhere: the doctors and nurses, the compassionate roofers, the two little old angels who delivered us to the hospital, and especially Petey, who saved our Roxy, our entire world.

1983

EL PILON, THE EXTRA ONE

You are more than enough. - Me, to myself.

Dr. Ramirez is quiet after the exam. "I'll see you in my office," he says.

The nurse suggests I take a seat in one of two leather chairs in front of a glass covered desk. I scan the diplomas on the wall, some from universities in the United States, for completing conferences on the latest surgical techniques. I breathe a sigh of relief.

The doctor finally breezes in, shakes my hand, and takes a seat.

"How's your sister?" he says. "Christie, the one who came for your operation. And your husband?"

"Fine," I say. "All well." Get on with it. What's wrong?

He asks me how I feel and then, it's out. Cysts again. "You'll need surgery. And while we're in there, we might as well take the ovaries and your uterus," he says. "You won't be having any more kids."

"It's almost Christmas, I'm going to the US," I say. "Can it wait a few months?"

"It can," he says. "And while you're up there, get a second opinion."

I don't want surgery, so I look around for alternatives. I know an American couple in their 50s who swear that anything can be cured with acupuncture. I´ve got three weeks before I leave so I schedule an appointment every day. For an hour they poke pins into key energy spots all over my body and jiggle them around. I don't feel any different.

I cram the car with newborn clothes, a wind-up swing, and a wooden playpen, drive around the block, and unload my dreams for a third baby at the Salvation Army Orphanage.

We celebrate the holidays in New Jersey and, after packing away Christmas, I call and make the dreaded appointment with my sister's gynecologist.

After a two-hour wait, a receptionist shows me to one of this doctor's six examining rooms. He breezes in and, after a ten-minute exam, confirms the grapefruit-size cysts on my ovaries and the need for surgery. "But an operation would kill the baby," he says.

My eyes bulge.

"You didn't know?" he says. "You're pregnant."

I want to hug this man, grab him and twirl, but that would be inappropriate. They have "personal space" here. Instead, I lock my arms across my chest and laugh.

1983

VACATION FROM HELL

Loving you was like going to war; I never came back the same. - Warsan Shire

"It'll be fun," Sonny says. "A road trip to the Yucatan."
But he's not going with us. He's sending me and our two
toddlers, Petey and Roxy, with Robert, his best friend.

Robert is a twentieth century Don Quixote, half-crazy
for adventure. When they were in their early 20s, Robert
and the gang kidnapped Sonny on the day he was to marry
a girl who claimed falsely that she and Sonny would soon
be parents. Then, a few years later, Robert convinced a
few friends to explore some back roads, looking for
excitement. At a turn in the dusty road, they were
ambushed. One of the bandidos shot Robert in the leg.
Nearest hospital was half a day of hairpin curves away,
and by the time Robert was carried in, his leg was twice
the normal size with infection so advanced he lost his leg
just above the knee. This, however, has not dampened his
vagabond spirit, and he'll be driving.

"You're in good hands," Sonny says.

We agree to meet Sonny in Palenque after his tour with the orchestra. He'll fly down.

Pete and Roxy love the yellow VW bus; they each claim their own special seat.

A few hours on the road Robert points to the cooler between the two front seats: "I've packed some drinks."

I dig deep in the cubed ice. "There's nothing but beer," I say. "Maybe a hundred."

"Exactly," he laughs. "Gotta keep hydrated."

Mile after mile Robert gulps his beer and I plan our escape. The road stretches straight for miles, it's mesmerizing and Robert drifts into the opposite lane. I scream as we swerve in time to miss an oncoming passenger bus.

"Stop!" I say. "We're getting out."

"Aren't you having a good time?"

"Please stop drinking! You're going to kill us."

"You need to relax," he says. "Cheers!"

After 24 hours of nerve-wracking, near-misses, we finally rendezvous in Palenque with Sonny, who's refreshed and excited about the pyramids.

"How could you have let us go with that maniac?"

"You're fine. Relax. Let's just have a good time."

In Cancun, we pick up Robert's sister Alicia, her eight-year-old daughter, and Robert's mother from the airport. We're now seven people crowded into the Volkswagen bus.

We're on the road that runs parallel to the beach, so close we hear the waves breaking. It's pitch dark, no moon tonight, humid jungle thick up to the edge of the highway. I worry we might hit a wild animal or fall into a hole.

There are no painted lines and roads could just end with no warning. Just south of Tulum we hit something. Robert and Sonny get out to investigate and return beaming, with a dead *tepezcuintle,* the clean-cut cousin of the wild boar. Robert delivers it to the chef at the thatched-roof, open-air restaurant on the beach, where we camp for the night. Noon the next day, the pork-tasting kill of the previous night is served up with salsa and tortillas.

PETEY, ROXY, LAURIE, SONNY, ROBERT

Robert and his family stay in a cinderblock room of the only hotel on the beach, while Sonny, the kids and I sleep in a tent. I'm five months pregnant and twist and turn all night. The hard sand is uncomfortable, and I worry the kids might sleepwalk, wander off into the jungle, or meet the same fate as the tepezcuintle.

If the nights are difficult, the days are a nightmare. Robert and Sonny pass the hours swinging in hammocks, drinking and smoking, while I run after the kids. Roxy, at three is an explorer. She needs to know what is in those empty hotel rooms. I'm thinking pervert, kidnapper, homicidal maniac. Intrepid Petey, four, is drawn to the ocean like a killer whale to an otter feast. I imagine him swept out to sea, flailing, sharks circling. If I want my kids to have freedom, I'm going to need some help.

I'm with Petey at the water's edge and glance back to check the beach bums in the hammocks watching Roxy. She's gone. I grab Petey, drop him next to Sonny and run to find Roxy. When I turn, a wave is knocking Petey around, Sonny swinging in the hammock, passing another

SONNY, ROXY, PETEY – TULUM.

beer to Robert. When I insist that Sonny help me with the kids, he tells me to stop worrying; I'm ruining everyone's vacation. He doesn't think the ocean is a problem for a 4-year-old and the hotel is abandoned except for us. "No danger lurks in those rooms." He's not going to run after kids. He's on vacation!

"Where's Petey? Where's Roxy?" Robert mimics again and again. "Ha-ha!"

I do everything in my power to ensure that Pete and Roxy aren't swallowed by a whirlpool or dragged off down the beach by some child molester. I refuse to lose one child so Sonny can value the others. This is exhausting, so I decide to cut the trip short and fly home with the kids. Sonny and Robert can ride back together. They deserve each other. How long can I wait for Sonny to "find himself?" How long until I get some help?

1977

A LOSS UNBEARABLE

My life closed twice before it's close- It yet remains to see
If Immortality unveil a third event to me
So huge, so hopeless to conceive As these that twice befell
Parting is all we know of heaven And all we need of hell
                                                    Emily Dickinson

The call comes in late August. Christie whimpers from a
tiny apartment somewhere in Washington, D.C. "They
were at a rest stop, on the way home from camping...Mom
collapsed... a coma...maybe a stroke."

"Should I fly home?" I ask, hoping she'll say no. I've
just landed my dream job in the violin section of a
symphony orchestra in Mexico. Just fallen in love with
Sonny, a bass-playing, Mexican, Charlton Heston look-
alike.

"Mexico is so far. So expensive for you to fly. I can't
go to New Jersey...my job...husband." She's barely
coherent. "Just wait. I'll let you know."

A month later, I'm tiptoeing behind Dad into Mom's

antiseptic-reeking hospital room. She's asleep on her back.
Dad paces back and forth to the rhythm of beeping
machines, then stops to gaze out at the moonlit bay
beneath the third story window. On the horizon I see the
twinkling lights of Ocean City, pulsating with life,
unaware of a tragedy so overwhelming everyone should
drop to their knees.

"I've lost my bride," he wheezes. There are no tears.
He is unable to empty his sorrow, so deep is his grief. "I'm
lost without her."

I hold his trembling frailty. Words clog my aching
throat.

"I told them not to give her blood thinner. It would've
restored the flow of blood, but then maybe she'd
hemorrhage," he looks down, twirls his wedding ring.

Would it have made a difference?

The hospital sends her home. Mom needs pills and
injections, sponge baths, Kotex. Clara shows me how to
blow into the tube threaded through Mom's nose, a
stethoscope pressed to her stomach. "Listen for bubbles,"
she says. "Make sure you don't pour formula into her
lungs." Usually Clara (15) or Henry (16) do it. They're in
high school, still dependent on Dad. They have no choice.
I'm here for a 3-week visit. I get to go back to my
paradise. But guilt is already gnawing at my brain for
even thinking of abandoning my youngest siblings, Lia
(13) and Phoebe (11). George and Ana are off at
university. It wouldn't be right to ask them to sacrifice an
education to care for Mom; she wanted us all to have a
degree. Doctors say the brain damage is permanent.
Maybe we can take turns.

Dad drags over to Absegami High School every day to face English and Spanish students, whose biggest worries are making the football team or a finding a date for the prom. Dad is fighting soul-suffocating depression, but he needs to work. Phoebe, the youngest, has six years left before she graduates from high school.

Thursday evenings, someone from the Methodist Church, where we never missed a Sunday in fourteen years, shoves an arm holding a steaming dish through the back door. No "How are you?" or "Do you need anything?" or even, "So nice of you to play violin in church last week." They dash away, as if heartache is contagious.

Over the next few months, my sisters send letters of Mom's progress. She is regaining consciousness and strength but is now a nightmare of responsibility. Her mind gone, she's a toddler on the loose in a 52-year-old body. Overstuffed chairs and couches reek of urine; Dad nails metal bars to all the windows in the house and all the doors are locked. Someone hides the key in a new place; a fire and we're all dead.

Mom swallows cleaning fluid she finds under the kitchen sink, she lights fires in her closet and the trash can. They hide poisons, matches, and knives but she finds them.

"Mom's missing!" someone yells, and they spring from the house in all directions, frantically combing the quiet middle-class neighborhood. The police find her wailing, arms flailing, in the middle of a busy intersection. "You need to take better care of her," one officer says when they bring her home. "Or she'll need to be put away."

But Mom's always looking to escape. One

Thanksgiving, celebrating what little joy we can muster, Mom sneaks up to the second floor, finds an unlocked door, and jumps out a window into bushes, suffering a bruised hip. Another day she flees to Phoebe and Lia's school, where she worked as school nurse. She´s looking for her office. My younger sisters watch in horror as she runs through the hall shrieking, in a green knit hat, baggy pants and ski jacket.

Guilt is unforgiving, and I fly home often. One day, on my watch, I find Mom with a butcher knife, prying hinges off a locked door. I peel her fingers off the knife but, not quick enough, she smacks my hand onto the blade, slicing my first finger to the bone. Dad drives me to the hospital for stitches, begging me not to tell anyone. "The police will come for her," he says.

The hell of helplessness and despair is choking the life from my siblings. "We found an affordable Catholic nursing home: Sisters of Mercy," Clara writes. But two weeks later, her report is tragic. Mom is back home. The Sisters had wrapped her in a straight jacket tied to her wheelchair tethered to a pillar next to the nurse's station. Drugged semi-conscious. "Mom didn't get much mercy from those Sisters. Seeing her like that smothered the last flicker of life from Dad. We can hear him sobbing night after dark night."

"We just can't do it anymore," Dad says, on the phone. "Five years of infernal misery. We're worn out. Could you please consider watching your Mum?"

"Of course," I say. We have a four-year-old and a three-year-old. I don't even consider the emotional strain on Sonny or our kids. Guilt, for not doing my share, has been following me like a tailgating semi. Here's my chance to exit and find some relief.

Clara and a friend fly Mom to Mexico City. Leaning on Clara, she pushes her way through the Mexican immigration stall. "*Enferma, enferma*," sick, sick, Clara mumbles. The officials point to the nearest bathroom, Clara's friend fills out paperwork.

Mom rooms beneath our loft nest, and we wake several times a night to screeching and rattling of wooden doors.

"I married you, not your mother!" Sonny says, after two weeks of sleepless nights. "Someone's gotta go. Your mother or me?"

The next day, Sonny says he's sorry. "It's rough when we can't sleep," he says.

I scramble for solutions and hire Martha, an older lady from the village, to care for Mom. Then, I schedule an appointment with a psychiatrist. The doctor asks questions and Mom responds with high-pitched howling, pointing an accusing finger at him. I told him she can't talk or reason. We leave with a prescription for phenobarbital to help her sleep.

I hate giving my mom injections. I only just learned to do this from watching my neighbor. Mom is paper thin and I'm afraid I'll hit bone. The medication fails, the nocturnal racket continues, and so I stop the needles. We move Mom to the little house and hire Isaac, a young man from the village, for the night shift.

Mom knows she's not in New Jersey; she doesn't try to climb the chain-link fence surrounding our property. My biggest worry are the kids. If Petey or Roxy, wander too close with cookies or a baby doll, she grabs their hair with one hand and snatches with the other. "Why does she do that?" they sob. "She's a grownup."

I'm healthy pregnant but worry that wrestling with Mom in the shower might hurt the baby. Martha and Isaac restrain her, but she thrashes lose and hits me hard in the face and stomach. She doesn't mean harm, she's just cold and wants her clothes.

Dad writes letters of encouragement all year and visits in the summer. Mom drags him to the couch and hugs his arm for hours. Does she know that he's her husband, or even what that means? We don't know what she knows.

The second summer, Mom smiles and claps to welcome Dad back. This time, when he leaves in the fall, she's heartbroken. "Harrow, Harrow!" (Harold, Harold) she cries for days. It's the only word she can say after seven heartbreaking years. As weeks pass, she loses interest in food, and finally she won't leave her bed. Now she won't eat at all, clenching teeth when she sees a spoon. The doctor shows me how to insert the needle for the saline drip. I don't know if it stings or if she's given up on life, but she yanks the needle out if I don't tie both arms to her bed. My heart aches to see bruises on her bone-thin arms.

My little ones need to be rocked, they need bedtime stories and violin lessons. The builders of our two-bedroom addition need to know where to put the stairs, what kind of roof tile I want, who's picking up the extra bags of cement. Life drags me along.

Carmen, my nearest neighbor, and I are on the front terrace having midday tea. There's hooting from a low branch in the pine tree next to Mom's house. "How long has he been there?" Carmen asks, shading her eyes. "Owls sense when death is near."

The dogs are restless, circle the trees and sit at my feet, panting on my legs, pawing now. I don't want to believe it. "How is it they know?" I say.

I call Dad. "Please, don't plug her in," he says. "Don't prolong the suffering."

MY PARENTS' WEDDING PICTURE

"Allow events to unfold naturally," the minister says. He hands me a book with the steps for "successful grieving." I feel nothing.

It's Saturday night. Sonny is playing a concert in Mexico City and won't be home until tomorrow afternoon. The caretaker has the day off, so the kids and I are alone, the nearest neighbor a half a mile away.

We pile into the king-size bed, read a story and drift off. At midnight I slip out from between dreams to change the drip. Moonlight floods the room where Mom is sitting up, shrieking, arms thrashing. I switch on the lamp, sit and hold her. "I'm here. What's wrong?" We rock together, calm now, breathing slow and shallow. I lay her down. A blank stare. Her body jerks. All is still.

She's gone. I hold her hand, yearn to feel her spirit take flight in some magnificent, unique way, the same way she'd lived. Mating cricket's hum in the darkness. Life can't be bothered. Bending over Mom, holding her, my tears wetting her cheeks, I say a prayer. May her noble spirit mesh into divine Love and Light. Finally, she's at peace, her soul released from a broken, traitorous mind. Then, gratitude. "You always put your family first," I tell her. "You cherished us."

It's 2 o'clock in the morning, December 5th. No car, no phone. There's nothing I can do until daybreak. As I slip under the covers Roxy sits up: "*Oigo el corazón de abuelita en mis oidos,*" she says. "I hear Grandma's heart in my ears!" Twice more she repeats it, then lays back to sleep. You're leaving us. I want to feel you. She does. Please. Something.

At daybreak, the kids and I trek through the woods in wrinkled pajamas and matted hair, to the neighbor's phone.

"I'll come if you need me," Dad says. "But I'm worn ragged."

Next, I call Sonny. "I have to work," he says. "See you tonight." Sonny is burned out also. I can't blame him. He grumbled, but never left my side; always kept me going. Last, I dial the undertakers. They'll stop by later.

"The crematorium is shut down for repairs, so we've come for the body," one of the two young funeral reps says when they arrive. They lean against the station wagon, waiting.

My dear sweet mother is now "the body." I shake my

head, tears blurring carpenter ants burning a path through the yard. "We'll keep her here until it's time," I snap. They fumble off into the background, unwilling to argue with a sleep deprived, aching soul.

Neighbor Carmen bathes and changes Mom, then arranges *Alcatrazes,* calla lilies, in vases and lights 20 votive candles on the floor around Mom's bed. Such a simple, comforting gesture.

Henry, my brother, can't get a flight until the next day. By then, the pine box seems to be nailed shut but later, as two men load the coffin into a light blue station wagon, the lid slides. No one else notices. Henry is saved; death's dreadful reality shared only with me.

Sonny and Henry follow the station wagon to the crematorium in Mexico City, two hours away. I'm too exhausted to go.

1984

COMFORT FROM BEYOND

*The death of any loved parent is an incalculable lasting
blow. Because no one ever loves you again like that.
- Brenda Ueland*

My mother is dead. People stream in and out with flowers,
tequila and advice. I'm sick of talk about grieving and
what to expect. What I actually feel I don't dare tell
anyone.

     I accept Patty's invitation to be an extra in an
American movie filming at an old sugar-cane plantation,
Hacienda de Vista Hermosa, in the south of the Mexican
state of Morelos. Will it be a documentary about the
Spaniard's land-grab and barbaric treatment of the natives?
I hope not, I need a break from suffering.
    "Come with me," Patty says. "I'll take you away."
She's Pastor Bob's wife. I trust her.
    The director assigns 15 of us to round tables in a

restaurant that was once a stone-walled, tunnel-shaped warehouse. Candles flicker from castle-chic chandeliers. I'm transported back centuries and for five days we pretend.

But I'm obsessed with thoughts of our kids: What possessed me to leave my babies? Will Sonny get them out of the house if it collapses in an earthquake? Why didn't I tell him where I stored the rattlesnake anti-venom?

On the last day of filming, two American actresses (cleavage, platform shoes, dark roots) hitch a ride back to town.

"What's the movie about?" I ask the one with pumpkin-orange lipstick. "We're not allowed to ask any questions."

"They don't tell us either. We just do the sex scenes," she says, as if it were as normal as grooming a dog. And then to her friend, "They better give us extra for that session out by the pool, when we did that Spanish *conquistador*."

Just drive. Eyes on the straight line.

"Hi Mom," the kids yell, banging a pinecone-filled plastic bag piñata hanging from a low branch. They're too busy for a hug.

"I gave up time with family to do a porno movie," I tell Sonny. "That's messed up."

"We're glad you're back," he says.

The kids and I are at friend Jodi's when suddenly I'm short of breath, my heart races, a sense of impending doom paralyses me. Jodi watches the kids while I melt in her bed.

"I had a panic attack," I tell Sonny. "I don't know what's the matter with me."

"You're just worn out," he says. "A change might be

good. Why not visit your brother in California?" He holds me and I sob into his neck. "You need time," he says.

I book a cheap flight to Tijuana. Somehow, I'll cross the border to La Joya.

The Mexican man next to me on the plane is chatty and handsome. He's about my age, slick, jet-black hair, sparkling-white smile. Somewhere over Sinaloa, he asks if I'd like to do some coke in the restroom. "I do it all the time."

"I've never done it," I say.

"Now's your chance," he winks.

Why not? I think, and follow him down the aisle.

It's tight. I sit on the toilet lid and he leans against the sink and shows me how to snort white powder from a tiny silver spoon.

An older woman is waiting when we exit. "¡*Qué cochinos*! How disgusting!" she says. She thinks we had sex. Wishes she could.

My mother died in my arms. Grief makes a person crazy. Oh God, from a porno movie to doing coke with a stranger 35,000 feet over Mexico. What am I doing? Who am I?

"A friend in Tijuana is taking me to La Joya," my seat partner says, as the plane bumps onto the runway. "Want a ride?" The coke wizard offers to obliterate my past, we can pretend in blissful ecstasy. Of course I want a ride.

I gasp when I spot the waiting Suburban with tinted windows and body builders in the front seat. But coke-fueled euphoria trumps caution and I hop in.

It's obvious from the United States border guard's familiar welcome that these guys are frequent visitors.

They wave us through with a smile.

What if I'm riding with kidnappers or drug smugglers? If they find something at the fifteen-mile checkpoint I could be arrested. Thrown in jail; gone without a trace.

Not to worry, border patrol salute us this time. Who are these people?

We drive to their friend's mansion in La Joya. I call Henry, my brother, but there's no answer. My handsome host invites me to take a shower, "make yourself at home." Then, he brings me a green-blue, chiffon pant-dress. "You'll look great in this for the party tonight." Flattery and white powder erase my husband, my kids, my life. I hadn't planned on partying tonight, but the siren voices beckon. Just until I reach Henry. I'm floating in a watery world, grief's jagged edges finally softened.

At the party house a butler shows us into the dining area, chandeliers sparkling, sideboards waiting with coke and champagne. Finally, Henry answers his phone and, amidst the fracas of laughter and Jimmy Hendrix, blaring from giant speakers, I escape with my brother.

The next day I imagine it all a dream, but the dress lies in a sea-green crumpled mess in the corner. I'm restless, unsettled, like a possessed teenager on spring break, yet I still ache for sweaty hugs and kisses.

At Henry's I'm free to be. Just be. No sticky hands pushing and pulling all day and hopeful, tender hands smothering me at night. Henry is off to work early every day. I sleep in, walk the streets, and then wait for him with supper and stories of the sacred space of our childhood. He doesn't ever mention our mother.

The kids are bubbling-happy when I return from my visit to the US. But the garbage strewn streets, the bone-thin stray dogs, and the toddlers selling chicklets on street corners depress me. Besides, I miss speaking English. I miss adult companionship. I miss washing machines and telephones. Life could be better in the United States.

Then, over the next few months, things begin to fall into place: Dad invites us to live at our childhood home in New Jersey with him. "I'm so lonely," he says. "I lost my bride." The orchestra grants Sonny a one-year sabbatical to study in New York City, and a missionary family from Minnesota rents our house.

Our welcome at Dad's is dismal. Lia, a college student, wanders the house like a ghost, ignoring me, retreating into self-imposed solitary confinement. My siblings visit.

Clara, a recent college grad is angry: "You let our mother die," she says. "You should be in jail."

Phoebe, a teenager, and George, a med student, lay down the law: "Don't expect us to watch your kids. You had them, they're your responsibility."

My father says to ignore them. "They're confused."

A few days after we arrive, I'm nauseous, my head throbs, ready to explode. I think stroke and tell Sonny, "No life support. Just let me go."

"Rest and let me know how I can help," he says. "We'll get through this."

Sonny is at my side with life-sustaining compassion. He bathes the kids and drives them to school, makes big pots of vegetarian stews, and holds me at night. He whispers: "What can I do for you? How can I help?" and patiently waits in the dark silence when sobbing is my answer.

As pounds drop off, doctors puzzle over normal lab results. They find nothing. In a month and a half, I've lost

30 pounds and the doctors' prognosis is cancer. My soul tells me it's not. I'm grieving, and no one links death with my body shutting down.

Mornings, I struggle to leave my bed to make sandwiches for the kids' lunches. They need to see "normal." It's all I'm able to do in a day.

"Where's Mommy?" they yell bursting in the backdoor, dashing to my bedside, little hands tight around my neck. "Please don't die," they whisper, burying their heads in my heart. At five and six years old they know I can disappear. They've seen it happen. My arms, my heart, my soul ache for them. Danny, two, is blessedly oblivious. Afternoons, Dad and Sonny fold laundry and take the kids to the beach. I'm unavailable.

Where is my faith? I weep, my spirit crushed. God has abandoned me.

I wander in a trance to the back door and peer out. The neighbor mows her lawn. Why does she bother? Then, memories of my mother invade my brain like demons flaunting the futility of life.

It's daybreak, Mom's already dressed, scrambling eggs on the stove and laying out 16 slices of bread for bag lunches. She drives us to piano lessons, dentist appointments, swim team meets, waiting until we finish to ask how it went. I boast to my friends that my mom is the school nurse. "She'll tell you if you need glasses." And every night she tucks each of her eight kids into bed with prayers for a better world, for comfort for those who suffer, and "please, take special care of Roxy." All she did. For what?

One especially dark day, I'm mysteriously drawn to the

basement. At the bottom of the stairs two green metal filing cabinets wait. I open a drawer and pull a smudged, worn file: Mom's letters written to her mother when we lived overseas in Colombia. She tells of desperate heartbreak when my six-year-old sister drowned. How she let little Roxy go to her best friend's birthday party at a public pool, how she regretted not taking the time to cut her hair the night before, the last thing Roxy asked of her. "How was I to know God was already calling?" she writes. She questions God's plan for her life; knows she needs to be strong for us, her treasures. It was a dark, dark time for us all.

MY MOM, FELICIA MAY HRBEK

Tears blur the shaking script. I pull another faded letter from the back of the drawer. Two years later, she describes how wonderful it is to be alive. "I love the fall, the crisp chill in the air blowing a heady, earthy perfume." Her children give her life meaning, she counts us as blessings and then explains how, with the gift of time passing, she has returned to a joy-filled life worth living.

Life has lost all meaning and joy for me. But now, here is my mother, reaching out, leading me to her letters, comforting me. She had walked the valley of the shadow, survived the loss, the unbearable misery, and so will I.

1983

AN ANGEL

Grant me the wisdom to rise to this sacred task of motherhood. - Me

Late August, a little after midnight, a red-hot poker pain jolts me awake. Contractions stable, I shake Sonny and we head for the hospital. But a few miles down the road I'm doubting. "The pain is coming every five minutes," I say. "But it barely hurts."

"What do you mean?" he says, banging both hands on the steering wheel. "You wake me up in the middle of the night and you're not sure? Where do you want to go? Home or the hospital?"

"Let's pull over and wait."

Sonny ignores me and drives to the emergency room. "I'm going back to bed. Good luck."

In the prep room five women in single beds are shrieking. "*Madre Santa de Dios, ayúdame!*" Holy mother of God, help me!" I can see the delivery room at the far end, an alcove the size of a large closet, a moaning woman on the examining table. She's surrounded by four young doctors, one up to his elbow inside the woman.

A nurse notices me watching. "Her water broke Friday," she says. "Here it's Monday and that baby isn't coming. We can't get a real doctor at these government hospitals on a weekend!"

Finally, a resident pulls a purple mass from between the woman's legs. The baby is limp, silent; the residents mumble, one whisks the baby out through a back door.

Pacing eases my contractions. A doctor bursts through the swinging double doors. "What are you doing here?"

"I'm having a baby," I say. "It helps when I walk."

He turns to the nurse and points a finger to the bed.

"Get those yelpers up!"

Trembling, I climb into the stirrups. Four effeminate men in white coats cheer me on. One pours a gallon of orange-red antiseptic between my legs. I hope there are no complications.

"What're you so angry about little blondie?" one says, ten minutes later, holding my screamer up to the light. "You stop that squawking."

"I want him," I say. He places a sticky, shrieking baby on my chest for a few seconds, then whisks him away. A blue gown wheels me back to a cacophony of painful praying.

A female doctor is making the rounds. "Are you over 35? Do you have three kids? If so, I'll schedule you for a free *Salpingo,* tubal ligation."

"This is my sixth kid," the lady in the next bed says. "We can't afford to feed any of them, but my husband thinks he's not a man if he can't have kids. He'd kill me."

"It's a tiny incision. He'll never know," the doctor says.

"I only have three kids and I'm doing it," I say.

By early afternoon the lady is convinced.

Hours drag on. By 5:00 P.M. I'm starving. "I don't want the operation," I say to a passing nurse. "Bring me tacos!"

Another blue gown rushes me through the wide swinging doors to surgery. As we roll, I'm doubting, for the first time. And then, last-minute bargaining to clear my conscience: God, if you want me to have more kids, send them another way.

Back in my room, my body aches for my baby. No nurses in sight, I sneak down the hall to the nursery. How will I know which is mine? On the other side of the window, nine copper-skinned babies, tiny heads thick with black down, dream in bassinets. Then I see him: red-wrinkled face, six strands of blond hair. This one's mine. My throat tightens, I weep and stare until I'm dizzy.

Back at my room a woman in a hospital gown and slippers is sitting on my bed. She's the mother of the purple baby.

"I saw you in the prep room," she says. "I had a boy." She stares at her hands. "He's dead," she says.

A tear wets her cheek as we sit in silence. She muffles a cough and then, head bowed, shuffles out.

She's taking nothing home. I am so sorry and so blessed.

The cysts disappear. Was it the acupuncture? The baby? A miracle?

I name our baby Daniel, after a boy I saw every day in band class in high school. He was perfect: shy, royal-blue eyes, soft voice. I imagined he would be honest,

trustworthy, loyal. He was everything. And he still is.
Because we never once spoke.

ROXY, PETEY, DANIEL

The name sounds like gentle strength but, as it turns
out, this baby needed a name like Godspeed. He's so
prone to tragedy that I consider dressing him in football
padding and helmet.

The day he's born a staph infection invades his tiny
body in blisters. He almost dies.

When Danny is barely a year old, I notice the lymph
gland in his armpit is red and swollen from an infected
splinter in a finger joint I never saw. It's too late for
antibiotics, the pediatrician tells me. "He could die." Three
men pin Danny on the examining table, while the doctor

lances the golf-ball sized abscess. Over Daniel's desperate screams, I beg the doctor to give him anesthesia.

"It won't take effect with that nasty infection," the

DANIEL

doctor says. "You let it go too long." Half a cup of green pus drains from the incision.

When Danny's two years old, he falls off the upper bunk bed and hits the back of his head on the windowsill. "I didn't think he'd fall off," Sonny says. "He was having such a good time bouncing around up there." Sonny doesn't mean to be careless. He's just incapable of gauging a potential catastrophe. So, knowing this, will the tragic outcome be my fault if I leave him with the kids?

"Some people don't deserve to be parents," the emergency room nurse mutters, as she scrubs the wound with gauze.

I'm doing the best I can. We all are. At one time, I believed that loving them, dedicating my life to them, would be enough.

Aunt Jo lives in Bayville, New Jersey. Her house is bordered on two sides by the bay, deep enough for boats to maneuver and dock. From the kitchen I watch Danny stack blocks on the living room floor when suddenly, he's gone. I run through the house, yelling his name, then out to the yard and along the edge of the murky green water, impossible to see past the surface. Maybe he wandered down to my cousin's bungalow, a block away, also on the water. I grab a bicycle and pedal frantically. Oh God, if he didn't, he's in the water! Oh God, he's gone! He's drowned! Get a grip. Accept it. My angel, you're gone. Tears mingle with salty sea air, stinging my face, as my legs spin, and I prepare to face the unimaginable. I throw the bike down and race to the bay side of my cousin's house. Sonny is chatting with my uncle, Danny in his arms.

Sobbing, I yank Danny away. "I've just lived a nightmare. Why didn't you tell me you were taking him?" My heart is pounding and I want to scream. I already lost a sister. What were you thinking?

"Relax," he says. "Nothing happened."

1985

A LAWSUIT

It is easier to ask for forgiveness than it is to get permission. - Grace Hopper

I don't sleep well the week before the meeting. Once again, I've been burned by people I care about.

Martha cooks and does housework and Isaac tends the vegetable garden and feeds the animals. They aren't related but come together daily from the neighboring village.

Danny is two months old when Martha´s third grandson, Manuel, is born. A week later Martha tells us, as emotionless as a TV newscaster, that her son has killed Manuel's mother. In an alcoholic craze he beat his wife to death. Officially, it was a stroke.

My heart drops. "Who's taking care of the kids?

"Martita," Martha says. "She's 12 years old."

"Bring the baby with you when you come to work," I say. "He'll sleep most of the time anyway."

I nurse Danny and have plenty of milk to feed Martha's grandson as well, even enough to send a bottle home for a night feeding. Holding him, I breathe in his black downy hair, stroke his smooth copper skin, kiss his pencil-thin fingers. Danny's hair is sparse and barely visible, his skin red-rough. I adore them both.

We try to convince Martha to let us adopt Manuel. I don't mention that we want to save him from growing up motherless with a violent alcoholic father. "You and your husband will always be the grandparents. You can visit whenever you want. See what your son says." But then, whenever I bring it up, she smiles and shakes her head. I doubt she's asked.

Maybe Martha worries I'm getting too attached because one day, when my babies are six months old, Martha arrives without her bundle.

"Sonny doesn't like me to bring him," she says, when I ask. "I think the crying bothers him. It's better if I leave him at home."

"It's not true," I say. "He's fine with it. Sonny even suggested the adoption!"

My chest tightens every day that she arrives empty handed. How can a twelve-year old care for three young kids? A month later Martha calls from the hospital.

"Please come," she says. "He's been vomiting with diarrhea for three days."

At the hospital Martha leads me to an incubator. He's convulsing. Dying. I sit in the waiting room and a few hours later he's gone. I can't breathe. Tears pool and drip.

I try to make up for the loss by bringing them clothes, tape players, watches, even binoculars from the US. But it's not enough.

Finally the day of the meeting arrives. Heat rises from my chest as I listen to Martha and Isaac's testimony at the government arbitration office.

"According to the defendants, you demanded 16-hour workdays, you never paid Christmas bonuses and you refused to give them days off."

"Why are you lying?" I ask.

Both crossed their arms, their eyes still fixed to the floor. The lawyer drones on about severance pay, fines for overtime, breaking the law.

"How can you say these things?" I say to Martha.

The lawyer pulls us aside. "They don't deserve anything because they haven't worked long enough. If you want, you can give them each a month's salary and be done with it."

We exchange pesos for signatures, and they're gone. I still ache.

"It's not about you," Sonny says. "We're the *conquistadores,* and they hate us, even if we treat them well. It's in their roots."

"We just have to keep doing what's right," I say. "And they know we are."

A week later, Martha is knocking at the gate. She's sorry, she needs work. I feel like we're under water; her words are blurry and she's surrounded in a yellow haze. I don't open the gate and stumble back to the house with a lump in my throat. Sonny is standing at the door watching me, mouth open.

"I said no," I say.

1985

TWO STEPS BEHIND

The whole course of things goes to teach us faith. Belief and love – a believing love, will relieve us of a vast load of cares. - Ralph Waldo Emerson

I wonder if I'm deserving of motherhood, if I'm doing all I can to nurture these tender souls. At the grocery store, my kids hang on the cart while I scan labels for artificial colors or flavors. I agonize about dragging them on yet another cross-country odyssey. "You draggin' those kids all over the place is gonna make for some unstable adults," Moses, a neighbor says. And no school is to my liking. Desks in strict rows and spirit-crushing teachers damage all kids' creativity. My kids are so innocent and vulnerable; I shudder to think of the evil lurking in the world. And then, life teaches me that I have little control over the divine plan for my kids, or over anything, for that matter.

One day, we take a walk in the woods surrounding our house. Roxy and Danny's sweaty hands squeeze mine on either side, and Petey blazes a trail ahead. Brush and fallen yellow and red leaves are thick, and I scan the ground for rocks and fallen limbs. Then, I gasp as Petey's little sandaled feet step over a rattlesnake the thickness of my forearms. I'm three steps behind deadly fangs.

"Stop, Petey!" I say, pulling Danny and Roxy back. "A rattlesnake. Don't move."

The rattle lies still. "Maybe it's dead," I say. "But don't come any closer. These guys are Olympic jumpers."

I toss a small stone, graze the tail and he wriggles off. What might have been.

My next lesson is a near-death experience with Roxy. It confirms that I'm neither in control nor alone in this sacred task of childrearing.

After her swimming class, four-year-old Roxy lies down on the sun-warmed cement walkway bordering the pool, three steps away from where I sit with sleeping Danny in my arms. The blond scorpion must have been hiding under a guava leaf. Roxy jumps up, holding her lip, screaming. The deadly insect scurries over the side of the pool. Ingrid, Roxy's swimming teacher, knows what to do. She dashes for the spice rack in the kitchen and whips up a thick paste from meat tenderizer. She slathers Roxy's lip in a white froth. "That will neutralize the poison and keep it from spreading," Ingrid, our angel says.

Two years earlier, Roxy was attacked by a pet puma. That time, we were visiting Norma in Mexico City, at the house where I'd lived as a university student.

Sonny, Norma, and I chatted around the picnic-bench kitchen table. She served us lemongrass tea and Philippine butter cookies. Norma's daughter, Vicky, was watching Pete and Roxy in the backyard. Suddenly Vicky, screaming, "Help us. Someone! Help!" We raced out the back door to find Roxy on the ground, the puma on top mauling her. The four of us pulled the puma from Roxy, and then he lunged for Petey. Norma grabbed the frazzled rope and dragged him away, hissing.

"The puma's fangs and claws were removed, so he's not dangerous," Norma said later. Roxy's face and arms were bruised and scraped, but the psychological damage was worse, and we noticed it as the days passed. Roxy chewed her nails during the day and ground her teeth at night. "That big cat only wanted to play," I said, when she asked about the puma. But it took months for the nervous ticks to disappear.

Then, it's Danny's turn to teach the lesson. It's dark by the time we finish our visit at a friend's house. Three-year-old Danny holds the railing, taking the steps one at a time ahead of us. But the minute he touches gravel, he bolts for the dark, right side of the house, barreling into the black unknown between the house and the street wall.

"Where are you going?" I call. "Come back!"

It's so dark, I've lost sight of Danny. And then, a scream. Muffled crying is coming from inside the earth. I drop and crawl and then, the ground drops away. Danny sobs from inside a hole. *How deep is it? Is there water? Is he hurt?* I swing my arm back and forth inside the pit.

"Do you see my arm? Grab it."

"I can't reach. Help me!"

I put my face to the earth, reaching deeper. "Can you see it now? Grab on!" Finally, his tiny cold hand grasps mine and I pull him out. He's soaked in blood, dripping from his head. How could people leave a hole this size uncovered?

Sonny drives us to the emergency room. As the nurse shaves Danny's head, she lectures: "It's the obligation of the parents to watch their kids!"

I was three steps behind him, I want to say. Sonny puts an arm around my shoulders.

I realize that my job is to care for my kids the best way I know how. I will love and cherish my sacred charges, and then let go.

ROXY, DANNY, PETEY

1985

THE PIÑATA

We cast spells when we speak to our children. -Laurie
The way we talk to our children becomes their inner voice.
- Peggy O'Mara

"Ready to go?" Roxy asks, standing in a beam of sunshine, sparkling with new-day hope. Her shoes are on the wrong feet, the five buttons of her yellow sweater one off, and her shoulder-length straw-blond hair a tangled, braided mess.

"Of course I'm ready, love," I say, gathering her into my lap. I knew this day would come and my heart aches. I've debated for weeks whether to go along with the centuries-old, unchallenged tradition of my adopted country or forbid my kids to participate in the barbaric custom of the birthday piñata. But it's not even up to me. Insidious undercurrents have already seeped into my daughter's crystal soul. Schoolmates, teachers, my own father casually ask Roxy what kind of piñata she wants, assuming we will participate. She's been swept away.

I slip off the rubber bands and run my fingers through

the knots in her hair. She pushes my hands away, and wiggles to the floor. It's Roxy's fifth birthday and she's anxious to pick out her own piñata. What does that even mean to a small child?

The spectacular piñatas can only be found in Mexico City, two hours by car, so we're going in. My daughter deserves the best, or at least a fair number of options for whatever it is she can imagine beating to death.

When the Spaniards invaded Mexico in the 1500s, the friars who tagged along introduced the piñata. It was a seven-pointed star, representing the seven deadly sins. Pounding the piñata with a stick represented man's dominance over those sins and the candy that spilled out was the reward for following the righteous path. And how better to represent unquestioning faith in the teachings of the Catholic religion, then with a blindfold.

What sins can my innocent one, humming in the back seat, be guilty of? Her head still swirls with fairy tales, where good triumphs over evil and there's always a happy ending. Do I tell her what it's really like? *No one ever told me.*

The shops in the downtown piñata zone burst with brilliant colored Superheroes, dinosaurs and giant stars. Roxy is in wide-eyed awe, but shakes her head time and again.

"We need to start for home soon," I say, four weary hours later.

Suddenly, eyes blazing, face flush, she points to the piñata-packed shelf behind the clerk of the last shop on the last block. "There it is," she says.

Wedged between a pink burro and a gold shining star, in the farthest corner of the shop, a black pig stares at us.

He's as large as Roxy.

"Are you sure that's the one?" I ask, as the clerk dusts off the pig and sets him on the floor.

"Oh yes!" she claps, then throws her arms around his neck. "It's Wilbur, from Charlotte's Web."

How will she feel when her guests smack the cherished pig with a stick, when they dive in to tackle the prizes raining down from his brokenness, trampled toddlers crying, mothers cheering their greedy offspring. There's always heartbreak. What will it do to her?

I'm sweating. A deep breath.

And then I see it: Roxy stepping carefully through the strewn pieces of Wilbur, offering hugs and chocolates to the sobbing little ones who got nothing.

"It's OK if you don't want to break Wilbur at your party," I say. In the rearview mirror I watch them in the back seat. She's kissing him now.

ZACH, ROXY, THE PIG, LORE, DANIEL, PETEY, GIACCOMO

1986

ORCHESTRA DRAMA

God, grant me the serenity to accept the things I cannot change, courage to change the things I can, and wisdom to know the difference. - Reinhold Niebuhr

Sonny leaves for work and I nurse baby Danny, pick up toys and feed diapers through a wringer washing machine. I practiced violin eight hours a day so I could do this?

Sonny encourages me to go back to work, but I refuse to leave the kids with anyone until Danny's three years old. "These are the most important years of his life," I tell Sonny. "Not enough love and he'll be damaged forever."

Time passes quickly, and at the end of Danny's third summer, I'm ambivalent about returning to professional life. Only I can give the kids the care they need, but at the same time I miss playing great music and I'm starved for stimulating conversation with people over three feet tall.

"Orchestra rehearsals are only in the mornings and then only two concerts a week," Sonny says. "You're not abandoning them."

"I want somebody like Mary Poppins."

"Good luck," he laughs. "This is Mexico."

Within a week Julie arrives. She can live at our house during the week but needs to bring Eliza, her two-year-old daughter, to work. I hesitate. Sonny hires her.

SONNY, LAURIE, JULIE

It feels good to be back performing a new program every week with world-famous soloists and guest conductors. But there are some behind-the-scenes issues that bother me. First, we aren't considered "professionals," as the professors are, because most of the orchestra musicians never graduated from university. We're "workers" and have the same status as the people who mop the marble floors or sell season tickets. That means everyone has access to backstage dressing rooms. One day, while I'm in the shower, my shampoo and sweater disappear from the bench outside. I report the theft to the manager, but nothing is recovered, and the situation worsens. The cleaning women shower and leave their bloody Kotex in the shower stalls. Forgotten jackets, lunches or coffee cups on stage or backstage are never seen again.

One day, Sonny forgets his tux in the dressing room, and when he runs back from the parking lot it's gone. He finds the general manager of the hall and offers a reward.

"Who's going to want it?" Sonny says. "It's huge!"

In less than a week, the tux is in the manager's office, but he wants the $100 reward before he'll hand it over. Sonny insists on giving the reward directly to the person who turned it in. The manager refuses. While they argue I notice a singular mug on the manager's desk.

"There's my mug!" I say, snatching it. "Wow! What luck that you found it."

"That's my mug," he sneers.

"I bought it from an artisan in Alaska," I say. "Look, he even signed it for me."

"My aunt brought that back for me. She also went to Alaska."

Sonny gets his tails back without paying the reward, but the manager keeps my mug. And when he sees us backstage, turns and walks the other way.

It bothers me that some of the married men in the orchestra have girlfriends and brag about it. Saturday nights their mistresses accompany them to concerts and then, on Sunday afternoons, their wives and kids are in the audience. In each case, the mistress is proud to be "the chosen one." He's under no obligation to be with her. And the wife is content because she's the queen of his castle.

UNAM ORCHESTRA, NEZAHUALCOYOTL HALL

One day after a rehearsal, a group gathers in the parking lot. No lover or wife in sight, I speak my mind: "I'd leave Sonny if he ever cheated on me!"

Sonny just rolls his eyes and smiles.

"You American women destroy your families over any little thing," Enrique, a violinist, says laughing. "It's normal to have girlfriends on the side."

"You made a promise to be faithful," I say.

I look at Sonny. He gazes at the asphalt, jaw set.

"We are faithful," the violinist says. "We provide everything our families need."

"What about your wives?" I say. "Can they have lovers?"

"No," the timpanist says. "Our wives take care of us and our kids. They hold the family together. They have

DOUBLE BASS SECTION UNAM

no time to run around."

My mother warned me about this. Sonny was raised with this paradigm; his own father was a womanizer. Here, young girls watch their fathers and brothers come and go. They seem to have it all figured out. Who am I to argue?

The parking lot of the concert hall is not only a place for heated arguments, but a place for celebrations as well. We drink to guest conductors, soloists, newlyweds, newborns, retirees, new recruits, birthdays, Day of the Dead. The list never ends.

There's one lone tree in the parking lot where everyone congregates, so when they announce, "*Hay arbolito*", it's tree time and everyone knows it's party time. The host only opens the trunk of his car overflowing with food and alcohol and the fun begins.

My friend's birthday coincides with her first week in the orchestra. She takes a cake and coffee to the hall to celebrate at intermission. It's not in the tradition of *el arbolito* and the musicians let her know.

"We don't want fucking cake," a cellist says. "*¡Queremos chupar!*" We want to drink!

After rehearsals I'm always anxious to get home. I try to rush Sonny, but he likes to take his time packing up his bass and chatting with friends. We're always the last ones to the car and most days at least a few colleagues are gathered under *el arbolito*.

"Come have a drink with us," they call to Sonny.

"No, I have to get home," he says.

"*Mandilon!*" they laugh. A *mandil* is an apron.

Sonny smiles as he starts the engine. "I'd rather be with you any day," he says.

I sigh relief, but what will it take for him to cave to the whims of his peers?

Despite challenges with my colleagues, they are the ones who are with me the night of my epiphany.

At our meetings for worship during my childhood,

Quakers spoke of mystical experiences as being a state beyond the realm of ordinary consciousness, of unity with a superior power. I always thought those encounters were for spiritual heavy weights. But it happens one night to me, unbidden and unexpected.

It's our Saturday evening concert and halfway through Tchaikovsky's Romeo and Juliet, a surge of energy washes over the orchestra, ocean-wave powerful. In seconds I'm swept up by the music, my colleagues soaring with me. I'm one with the others, with the universe. The lush music swells, carries me. I am the music. Ecstasy. I'm powerless. I panic. I have to finish this piece, let me go!

At intermission, I'm sweating elated. I've just experienced the divine, manifested through music. Who else was caught up in this mystical moment? I ask the others backstage, eager to share. "No, not exactly," they say. It was beautiful, but nothing extraordinary.

Sonny is level-headed and easy going. Under his leadership, the basses boast the tightest section in the orchestra; they're as thick and defiant as a New York street gang. When the director arbitrarily fires Miguel on second stand, they all shave their heads. At the concert the public demands to know what has prompted such outrageous rebellion, and soon the story hits the local newspapers. The ousted bassist is quietly reinstated, and hair is left to flourish.

At home, Julie surpasses Mary Poppins. She's a cheerful, responsible caregiver for my kids, and her daughter Eliza is a perfect playmate. Julie takes them on walks to pick wild blackberries and mushrooms, reads them mountains of books, and teaches them how to make salsa. Then, in the afternoons she tidies up the house, while I homeschool.

I'm happy with my orchestra job and Julie but worry about the kid's education. In Mexico the schools are army-boot-camp strict: they stifle the questioning mind and smother the blossoming spirit.

"It doesn't matter where they go to school," Sonny says. "The important things they learn at home anyway, like returning the pony they 'borrowed' from the neighbors or reviving a starving puppy someone dumped out here on the mountain."

I don't agree and push for a move to the United States, where Montessori and Waldorf schools abound. But Sonny has no desire to leave his beloved orchestra, his high school buddies or his hot tacos.

BASS SECTION SHAVED HEAD SOLIDARITY

1988 THERAPY

When in doubt, love with abandon. - Me

It's my idea to go to therapy. "It's a marriage tune-up," I tell Sonny when he makes a face. In reality, I'm unhappy and disappointed. Expectations of what marriage and parenting should be, based on my own blissful childhood, were trampled years ago.

Elsa ushers us into her posh office, red plush carpet and matching velvet curtains framing a floor-to-ceiling window. After we're seated and introduced, she hands us each a pen and paper. "Write down everything that annoys you about your partner," she says. "You have ten minutes."

First, she asks me to read my list. "Sonny doesn't interact with the kids, doesn't pitch in around the house, spends too much time with his friends…" On and on I read, Sonny staring into his hands.

After I finish, Elsa turns to Sonny. He sighs, then says, "The only thing that bugs me about Laurie is, … she has that list."

My face burns.

"There has to be something," Elsa says.

"No, nothing," he says. "She's a perfect mother and a great wife. I didn't realize she felt this way."

"Men need instructions," Elsa says to me. "Do you tell him what you need?"

"I don't want to have to ask him for every little thing," I say. "The other day, I told him that it looked like rain and there was laundry hanging outside. I came home to a downpour, forgotten laundry dripping on the line."

"Men's brains function differently," she says. "They need details, lists. Otherwise, you're going to be wearing wet jeans the rest of your life."

"Say what you need and I'll do it," Sonny says.

1988

NICKNAMES

I love nicknames. It makes me feel loved. It makes me feel less alone in this world. - Ellen Page

No one can escape the blessing, or curse, of a nickname. It's part of the culture. A physical anomaly or a quirky personality trait will spark someone's creative genius; they will have an epiphany and you, a new name.

A week after starting classes at the conservatory, my name is gone, replaced by an affectionate tag. I'm *la Camarona*, The Shrimp. Whenever anyone approaches, my face burns red, just like a shrimp tossed into boiling water. I can feel the heat rise from my chest and spread into my cheeks as I watch lips move and try to piece together words I recognize into something coherent.

I prefer other nicknames. When Carmen learns I'm pregnant, she hugs the breath out of me, "Now we can be *Comadres,"* she says. She's decided to be our baby's Godmother, sealing our friendship forever. She'll never again call me by my given name.

One would think we work in a zoo instead of an orchestra. A long, narrow face and big teeth, they call Carlos, in the first violins, *el Caballo*, The Horse; others earn their nicknames from uncanny visages: *el Perro*, The Dog, *el Alce*, The Moose, *la Mojarra*, the red snapper fish (protruding lower jaw), and *el tigre*, The Tiger. We have *el Borrego*, The Sheep, (one can easily imagine his hair knitted up into a black cardigan), *Hombre Lobo*, Wolf Man, (a beard and moustache cover most of his face), and *el Perro Apache*, The Apache Dog. (He resembles both an Apache and a Scottish Terrier.

A violist's incessant talk about women and sex earns him the name *el Cachondo*, Horny One. He doesn't seem to mind.

The concertmaster loves to drink and, even though he's not Japanese, his sobriquet is "General Yo Shi Tomo." It sounds like Japanese but in Spanish means "General Yes-I-Drink".

The musician with hair to his waist, we call *el Pelón*, Baldy.

The directors aren't exempt from the creative labels the musicians think up. *La Pantera Rosa*, The Pink Panther, walks exactly like the pink cartoon character, and *el Tejedor de Milagros*, the Knitter of Miracles, appears to be making a blanket when he directs in minute, symmetrical hand movements, knitting instead musical miracles from the orchestra. *Abuelito Addams*, Grandfather Addams is twin to the character in The Addams Family TV show-- only the cape is missing. Sometimes the epithet is ruthless, as in the case of *el Condorito*, The Little Condor, bulging eyes and hooked "beak."

My favorite is Ofelia's tag. A female double bassist,

she began classes at an early age. The instrument was almost twice her size and when she hoisted it onto her shoulders, she became la *Hormiga Atómica*, The Atomic Ant.

Long face, big front teeth, Sonny is another horse, but not just any horse. He's *el Rocinante,* the noble, emaciated companion of Don Quixote of La Mancha. When I marry *el Rocinante,* I become *la Yegua*, the mare, and our kids are, logically, los Ponies.

1988

A CAUSE TO DIE FOR

A man who has nothing he is willing to die for has nothing worth living for. - Martin Luther King, Jr

Arriving at Plaza Mexico, a bull ring in downtown Mexico City, we're greeted by ambulances, fire trucks and empty police cars, officers across the street chatting and dining.

"Hot tacos! Hot tacos! Come get your hot tacos!" the vendors yell as they flip the sizzling meat and tortillas under greasy flickering light bulbs.

We join a group of friends dressed in black, carrying instrument cases, making their way to the stadium. Beyond the food stands forty or so animal-rights activists huddle in the chilly night, bearing placards: "It's Not Culture, It's Business;" on another, the picture of a bull vomiting blood.

"Hypocrites!" comes a voice out of the dark. "Musicians are supposed to have some culture, but here you are supporting a massacre!"

"Supporting what?" I yell back to Sonny, who struggles

with his double bass, the crowd swallowing him as they surge forward. "What are they talking about?"

"Just keep walking!" he shouts. "Get inside the stadium!"

A protester shoves a flyer at me. "Dirty Game," it says, with a drawing of a bull, arrows pointing to parts of his body. I pause under a light. "The bull's ears are filled with wet newspapers to impede hearing, Vaseline smeared in the eyes to obscure vision, cotton in the nose and the throat to hinder respiration. All this, plus shaved horns so the animal can't defend himself. Now the bull is ready to face the brave *matador,* the killer.

I can't read any more. I'm dizzy. We were hired to play the opera Carmen. The organizers didn't mention anything about torturing a bull.

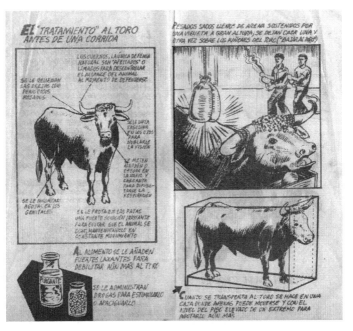

Two security guards nod as I brush past, my long black dress and violin my entrance pass to backstage. Emerging from a twenty-foot tunnel I look down to my left and notice a two-tiered flimsy plywood stage built into one side of the arena, the lower-level flush with the top of the barrier that secures the action to the ring. Huge stadium lights glare so brightly I see necklaces sparkling from the opposite, roped-off spectator section.

Taking my seat in the second violin section, I greet fellow freelancers from past performances with hugs and kisses. Catching up with old friends is the best part of gigging. A rumbling from above, I look to the sky to see the first of endless passenger jets on approach to the largest city in the world, so close I can count their tires.

The stage, inches above the trombones and clarinets, sags and creaks as Carmen seduces Don Juan. Then Jose, from the stand behind, offers me a thermos: "Go on, drink it. It'll warm you up." Obeying, I drink. The burning elixir can only be the best of Mexican tequila. "Pass it on!" he whispers. After another quick swig, I tap Victor. "No thanks," he says. "Not for me!"

The smell of rain, a few sprinkles, and then luckily the third act is over. A circle forms as we shuffle backstage, everyone babbling at once: "I'm not risking my violin. Not going out there if it rains." "What are we going to do if there's a real bull?" "They wouldn't have a bullfight during an opera! That's just crazy!" "The last scene takes place outside the bullring, not inside!" "Right! Jose kills Carmen in a jealous rage outside, while her lover, Escamillo is killing the bull inside. It's totally savage."

It's time for the Fourth Act. We gasp as a bull charges into the ring, greeted by cheers from the spectators. Then silence. The bull's heavy hooves and hoarse grunting echo through the arena as he circles the ring. Any sign of blood and I'll be needing that ambulance. Then, yelling. "No bull will die tonight." It's Victor. A shimmering aura surrounds his silhouette.

NI OPERA NI CORRIDA

ioble asesinato en la semivacía Plaza México. Las víctimas fueron *Palomo*, burel de 4 años ¡ 55 kilos, y *Carmen*, la obra maestra de Georges Bizet ■ Foto: **Fabrizio León**   ■ 2!

NEITHER AN OPERA NOR A BULLFIGHT

"Let the bull go or I swear I'll jump!" He's shouting at the edge of the stage, waving his violin in one hand, bow in the other, coat tails flapping in the wind. Another jet roars overhead. Is this really happening? What was in that tequila?

Panic creeps into the orchestra. My brain twists. I can't make sense of it. Victor, principal of the second violins, has crossed over into the double bass section and stands at the edge of the stage. "I'm jumping!"

126

Sonny grabs Victor's jacket, but he wriggles free.

Has Victor gone mad from that vegan diet? Or is this the tequila working some kind of spell on me?

The toreador rushes into the ring in his suit of sparkling sequins and gold braid, planting his feet just below the orchestra. "Get in here with me, you asshole," he yells, shoulders back, chest out, pants so tight there's no doubt about his masculinity. Eyes flashing, he screams at Victor. "Let's see how brave you really are!"

Three security goons tackle Victor to the floor.

"Leave him alone, you barbarians!" "Stop it!" "Take your hands off him!" we yell.

Blood-thirsty spectators from across the stadium join in: "Get rid of the tree-hugger!" "Don't pay the musicians!" "Bullfighter, kill the bull, kill the bull!" "Kill, Kill, Kill!"

Still in security's grip, Victor stands up, yelling across the ring, "Enjoy your spectacle, you murderers!"

Finally, the goons wrestle Victor to his seat.

"You'll finish this performance with no further interruptions!" one barks. The muscle men position themselves, arms crossed at the edges of the orchestra.

From the podium the conductor sighs, his nervous gaze sweeping the orchestra. "Turn your backs to the arena," he says. "We'll support our comrade by shunning this atrocity.

Even with our backs turned we know what's happening. *"Ole!"* the crowd cheers, each time the bull thunders by the *toreador,* who teases the bull closer and closer with his red cape. The *picador* enters on horseback and stabs the bull to weaken the neck muscles. Then *banderilleros,* dancing around, jab six short, barbed spears into his neck.

Breathless, we wait for the *matador* to thrust his long sword between the shoulder blades, severing the spinal cord and killing the bull instantly. But booing tells us that tonight he's an amateur and misses the mark. Several times. Some of my comrades weep openly. Finally, the bull is dead. From deep inside a nightmare, we play the final number, March of the Toreadors, while the *matador* circles the ring, waving to the applause of his fans. I hang my head. An animal was tortured and killed, and I did nothing but turn my back.

Packing up our instruments, someone behind me cries, "They're coming for Victor!"

"Which one of you tried to ruin the show tonight?" security man yells. "We want him for questioning!" Six more muscle men trot down the stairs and encircle us.

"No one is going anywhere!" the timpanist snaps.

"One goes, we all go," the second trumpet adds.

"He'll have to reckon with us sooner or later!" security says.

We sit motionless in our orchestra-assigned seats. After half an hour the alpha male breaks the silence, "It's over. Get the hell out of here, you fucking morons. Get out!"

We file out of the only exit, up steep narrow stairs running up between ten rows of bleachers, then through the tunnel emptying to the outside.

There's whispering: "This has been going on for years. It will never change." "Too many people enjoy it. Too many people make too much money from bullfighting." "Aztec sacrifices, where beating hearts were ripped from men's bodies, went on for over 200 years right here on this very spot, and that's changed. It's possible!"

Fresh air at last. But now, a woman rushes towards us,
"Who was it?" she screams. "Who the hell tried to ruin my
show? Tell me! Who was it?"

It's Paloma Brach, the producer. She throws an egg
from each hand and hits a trombone case and the backpack
of a protester. "I hate you!" she screams. And to her
henchmen: "Find that violinist who ruined my opera!
Bring him to me now!"

The activists applaud and, as we pass, shout
"Felicidades! Congratulations" They've heard about
Victor's pro-life incident. Cameras flash, reporters take
notes. The police keep their distance, staring from the
food stands. A woman screaming, eggs flying, animal
lovers dancing, placards bobbing, jets swooping, rain
sprinkling. A pulsating mass we reach my black, nine-
passenger van first. Super Animal, noble cause activist-
wrestler, is beside me. "Take him," he whispers through
his mask, as Victor and ten others pile in.

As I pull away, I notice, in my rear-view mirror, police
car lights flashing. I guess they've gotten their fill of
tacos. At every traffic light a few black figures hop out. I
don't know when I lose Victor, our hero.

What would I fling myself into a bullring for?

1987

PETE'S ORPHAN

Stop trying to make everyone happy. You're not tequila.
- Emmy Rossum

Eight-year-old Pete listens to the concert from atop a
waist-high wall at the back of the open-air auditorium at
Chapultepec Castle. He's leaning against one of the huge
white pillars surrounding the venue. One eye on the last
movement of Beethoven's 9th Symphony, another on Pete,
when my heart quickens. A shadow in rags approaches
from the right. A boy bends over, stares into Pete's face.
He's showing him something. Now he's taking him by the
hand. Leading him outside. Oh God, no. I'm lost. Did I
skip a line of music? Should I follow Pete and the
stranger? Notes and lines blur on the music I'm not
breathing. Finally, it's over. I run to find Pete, violin in
hand.

They're outside in the garden. The last rays of evening
reveal a boy not much older than Pete. "This is Carlos,"
Pete says, motioning to a thin, dirty waif, sunken eyes, dry

lips. "He has no mum or dad. He wants to live with us."

The boy's eyes are red and glassy. "*Tengo hambre*, I'm hungry," he slurs.

"After the concert we'll talk," I say. "Come sit up front, near the violins."

Sonny walks me to my chair. "He probably sniffs glue," he says.

"The least we can do is treat him to dinner," I say. "Encourage Pete's compassion."

At the restaurant, Sonny chats with the taco-guzzling boy. "Do you sniff?"

"Everybody does," he says. "It feels good."

"We can't adopt him until we know for sure he doesn't have parents," I say to Pete. "They might be worried."

I once read in the newspaper about a couple who adopted, only to find out months later that the mother still had a pulse. She sued for kidnapping. In another case, the adoptee let his cronies in the back door, and they helped themselves to everything but the grand piano.

In the phone book I find a government-run orphanage. The guard at the door won't let us in but will take the boy. The next day, Pete bugs me until I call. The receptionist has no record of Carlos. The guard on duty knows nothing. How does a boy disappear overnight? Pete cries. My heart aches. "It's for the best," Sonny says.

1988

POLICE DEALS

Though the bribe be small, yet the fault is great.
- Edward Coke

"In the United States you have the police big-brother enforcing laws," my friend Carlos says. "You're like kids, parents punishing you for every little mistake. Here in Mexico we can negotiate the law like adults." I know exactly what he means.

We're winding down the mountain, on the last curve into Mexico City when I see red and blue flashing lights in my mirror. Another cop on a motorcycle pulls alongside and motions me to the curb.

"You don't drive today," the officer says approaching my window in his knee-high black leather boots and skin-tight riding pants. He doesn't take off his helmet or his Ray Bans.

My five-year-old Danny is crying, Pete and Roxy, in the back seat, gaze wide-eyed at the lights and sirens of police vehicles surrounding us. "It's going to be OK," I say. "I'll handle it."

Because of severe air pollution, everyone is forbidden to drive one day a week, according to their license plate. My number is today.

"I forgot it was Wednesday," I say, heart pounding. "I'll just turn around and leave the city."

"Can't do that," he says. "Other patrols will stop you. We're taking your van to the pound."

It'll be days of paperwork and a steep fine if we go that route.

"Please, I'm on my way to Texas," I say to my reflection. "My father is sick. I forgot."

Two more uniforms approach and stare at sobbing Danny.

"What if I take my plates off," I say. "No one will know what my number is."

"That's a good idea," tight pants says. "We'll get our screwdrivers."

I get out and watch from the sidewalk as they unscrew my plates. I can't believe I just made a deal with a policeman. How easy it was to step over my integrity boundary.

"We're helping you out," one says, handing me the plates and screws. "What are you going to do for us?"

"I only have three hundred pesos (thirty U.S. dollars). I pay everything with my credit card."

"That'll do fine. Don't forget to put the plates back on at the toll booth north of the city."

My sweaty hands grip the steering wheel as I turn onto the Periferico, the north-south highway skirting the western side of the city. At every entrance ramp a motorcycle cop waits for easy prey. I cruise along in the passing lane and an hour and forty-five minutes later, Petey helps me screw the plates on. He saw it all:

I negotiated. I broke the law. What can I possibly say? How much do I have to give up of me?

1992

DEADLY HIGHWAY

One life; a little gleam of time between two eternities; no second chance to us forevermore. – *Thomas Carlyle*

A crack like lighting, sparks fly from the modem next to my computer and then, silence. Another crash, I think, as I race from the house and down the dirt road to the highway. Sure enough, two cars are stopped, and curious onlookers surround an overturned truck covered in a web of wires from a downed cement light post and a wooden telephone pole.

I dash back home for my camera and, by the time I return, a wailing ambulance, blue and red lights spinning, is parked on the shoulder. Two paramedics in bright orange vests direct traffic at the hairpin curve, above the accident. Fifty-gallon plastic drums, littered all over the highway, leak a suspicious green liquid. An onlooker unscrews the rearview mirror from the truck, another the radio, the jack and tarps.

My neighbor also notices: "He's from Tres Marias.

Has a parts shop up there. Take pictures, take pictures!"
he says.

I snap a few photos and approach one of the
paramedics, "Was anyone hurt?"

"There were only two men in the front seat, and they
survived," she says. "One of them will probably lose an
eye. They were lucky."

"Who is this guy that's loading his truck with parts from
the accident?" I ask.

"I heard one of the guys in the cab ask him to watch the
truck and take care of his things," she says. "Usually
passersby steal everything."

The last accident had been a tractor trailer, which
flipped over in this exact spot. An evangelical pastor and
his crew were on their way to a religious revival, a circus
with a spiritual twist. Books were scattered everywhere,

pamphlets blowing about in the breeze. I picked one up: "How to live with integrity, how to love unconditionally." The police weren't interested in the spiritual tracts. They were dragging tables, chairs, computers, even a huge canvas tent, back into the woods. Later, under cover of darkness, they returned for their cache.

"How can some people take advantage of another's misfortune?" I ask.

"That always happens at the scene of an accident," the paramedic replies. "We're used to it. Once we found people pushing an unconscious man out of the way to grab cans of tuna fish from underneath him!"

Trucks travel 20 miles of steep down-grade by the time they reach the entrance to our little dirt road. Hot brakes, a 45 degree turn and trucks flip, dumping loads of V8 juice, glue, cement, and eggs. Every time, people scramble for the goods, like kids diving beneath a smashed piñata to grab all they can. One man told me that if he didn't steal what he could, then others would do it; wouldn't it be stupid of him to let that happen?

One day, while waiting for the bus on the other side of the highway, I watch, with mouth open, as a red Volkswagen Beetle, coming too quickly for the curve, flies up into the air, completes two somersaults and lands upright in front of me. I'm sweating. Two men emerge, mumbling and stumbling drunk. I ask if they want me to call for help, waving my cell phone, but they shake their hands no as they circle the car, assessing the damage. After a minute, they jump in and head back up the hill from where they'd come.

There is only one cross at the crash site where our dirt road meets the highway. A large Coca-Cola truck,

winding up the road to the village met with a pickup truck
loaded with bags of potatoes rounding the curve too fast.
The truck flipped and dumped its load onto the cab of the
coke truck, burying the driver alive. Before the ambulance
arrived, villagers were already gathering potatoes in
wheelbarrows and pickup trucks.

COCA-COLA AND POTATO TRUCK ACCIDENT

Drunks, thieves, scavengers; this highway seems to
elicit the worst from human nature. One incident,
however, provides me the opportunity to teach my kids a
lesson about compassion and empathy.

That day, Sonny, the kids and I are playing cards on the
front porch when we hear screeching followed by a
monstrous thud. We dash for the highway and find a
passenger bus on its side, a few dazed women emerging

from the square emergency opening on the roof of the bus, about ten others staring as we approach. Sonny helps the women out, and learns that they are Girl Scout leaders from England.

"Where's the bus driver?" I ask.

"He's gone," says the tour guide in broken English. "The police will arrest him for questioning, so he ran."

"You appear out of nowhere," one woman says. "And

you speak English!" "You're angels!" another says. None of them speaks Spanish.

"You need to keep an eye on all your things," I say, as we help them gather luggage into a pile. "The police will be here soon, but just remember, you can't trust anyone!"

After about half an hour police arrive. First the municipal, then the state and federal. They surround the trembling Girl Scout leaders, pointing machine guns in all directions. I assure my new friends that the guns are for their protection, not directed at them. As if sensing their anxiety, the authorities lower their guns and back away. Then city, state and Red Cross ambulances arrive, and they argue about who will take the injured women. Peeking in the back I see that the ambulances are equipped with two long wooden benches and a first aid kit. That's it.

"Six women need hospital care," I say. "Everyone will get clients, but they need to go now." I ask that they deliver them to the government hospital where Danny was born. The women beg me to ride along. Sonny and the kids stay behind with the others to wait for personnel from the Girl Scout center.

At the hospital nurses and doctors flock to the new arrivals and I translate: some will be x-rayed and others sutured. Nurses hand me pocketbooks and jewelry to safeguard.

"The top of her head is a piggy bank," one doctor says to another. "But not for coins, for bills, to be inserted long-ways." I won't be translating this. Her skull is exposed, but luckily the wound is only skin deep. I hold the patient's hand and count 20 stitches.

Later, the Girl Scouts call to invite us to the International Center, one of four in the world, for the closing ceremony. My boys, Danny 6, Petey 10, and Sonny, 52, love the event where dozens of girls spin around them. Roxy and I also savor our hosts' appreciation. They view us us as an act of divine intervention.

The following year I receive gifts, along with invitations to visit England. The women send pictures of their homes and flower gardens, pirate coloring books for

140

the kids, and a book of English poetry. I would like to
believe they have good memories of Mexico.

1992

LIVING A LIE

One lie is enough to question all truths. - Anonymous

It's summer, 1992 and another family road trip, this time
to Michigan, my birthplace.

Great aunts and uncles, second and third cousins of my
paternal grandparents live around Fremont, a laid-back
farming community north of Grand Rapids. Main Street
is typical small-town USA: four blocks of coffee shops,
banks, and a Woolworth ending in a city park with a
gazebo. Not much has changed in Fremont since 1955,
when I was baptized in the Congregational Church, the
one out past the Gerber Baby Food Factory west of town.

We stop at the church. The door is unlocked and the
minister pokes his head out from an office off the foyer.
He greets us, thinks I'm here to apply for the position of
organist and/or youth activities director. I didn't even
know they were looking. This feels like a heaven-sent
nudge. It would be great for the kids to polish their
English. Maybe just for a year. I sign the contracts.

Sonny agrees and asks for a one-year sabbatical from

the orchestra. He doesn't really like the idea of wintering in the US; he'll miss hand-made tortillas, friends stopping by for coffee, and repairing violins and basses in his new wood shop. Therefore, he's relieved when the orchestra calls, denying his request.

PETEY

At first, we camp out on the lawn next to cousin Missy's house, a few feet from the dairy barn, where cows moo us to sleep, the rich smell of silage floating on pure country air. Missy has three kids, more or less the same ages as ours, 10, 13 and 14. She finds us a bungalow with a dock on a good-size lake. All summer, the kids swim in the dark-brown cedar water and paddle around in canoes. In the winter, under four stadium-huge spotlights, they play ice hockey until the moon is high overhead. Pete milks, feeds, and cleans stalls at Missy's 300-head dairy farm. I thrive playing the organ at church and first violin in the West Shore Symphony.

At first, I miss Sonny, but running kids to soccer practices, organizing activities for the youth program, and learning pedals for Sunday hymns pushes romantic longings farther and farther from my mind.

Sonny breezes in for a two-month honeymoon visit during Christmas vacation. At the end of January, he's flown off again. I don't worry about his scanty letters. No news is good news, Sonny has always assured me. But by March all communication stops.

On Good Friday a nightmare shakes me awake. I close my eyes and try to patch the fragments together. It's Sonny. He's walking away. Behind me the kids drift out to sea. They're crying.

How can I raise my kids without their father? Especially Pete, who's in seventh grade, a tender age to be fatherless.

One day, Mr. Romero calls asking for Pete's dad.

"I'm sorry, but he's gone back to Mexico," I say. "Maybe I can help you."

"I don't know what to do," Mr. Romero says. "I'm organizing the teams for the city soccer league, but no fathers on your son's team have time to coach. Your husband was my last hope. I hate to cancel the team. A lot of boys are going to be disappointed."

Pete will be devastated. "Don't cancel," I say. "If there's no one else, I'll do it."

"Great," he says. "See you at the high school Saturday at noon for the first practice."

The next day I stop by the library and check out eight

books on soccer. I know nothing about it and have only five days to cram. What am I doing? I don't even like soccer.

Eleven boys, hair slicked, with sparkling-white soccer cleats, kicking balls around, are already waiting when we arrive on Saturday. Pete has no idea I'm the coach.

Mr. Romero calls the boys into a circle, their fathers hovering nearby. "This is Mrs. Rodríguez, your new coach," he says, nodding my way.

"You know how to play?" one of the men asks, squinting.

"No, but I read some books on soccer," I say. "There's nothing to it. They just have to get the ball into that net down there."

"No one else volunteered to coach, except Mrs. Rodriguez," Mr. Romero says.

"I think we can arrange something," one of the dads says, gazing at the other men who nod their heads.

"Yes, we can take turns," says another.

The men make a schedule. I walk away, happy to watch from the bleachers.

I know that none of these men will replace Sonny. I'm cheating my kids by keeping them from him. They need their dad. I regret this move, but there's nothing I can do about these misgivings until the kids finish the school year and then attend the music camps they're signed up for. I'm on a mission to reunite my family and hope that the dry spell of paternal love and attention won't require therapy.

Finally, after three months without even a smoke signal, I call Sonny. How are you? Are you coming to the US for vacation?

"I'm going to a Sufi dance course in France," he says. "Javad, is teaching."

When I met Sonny, he was a vegetarian, a few years later, we were practicing Tantric sex, and now he's off to see his Sufi guru. "I have to be solid with myself before I can offer anything to someone else," he always preaches. When will nurturing his own kids' souls be a meaningful spiritual practice?

He wants me to meet him in Edinburg, on the Texas border, so he can say good-bye and I can give him a lift to Houston Airport. His voice is forced, polite.

Danny is excited about staying the weekend with Jose, his best friend from the years we lived in Texas. That will give Sonny and me some time alone. We meet for the first time in months at the empty house I still own in Edinburg. I tremble with excitement when I see him, but he steps back when I reach to hug. Silently we walk through the one-story ranch house, checking locked doors and windows, ending up in the orange-yellow shag-carpet bedroom Pete and Danny had shared.

"What's wrong?" I ask. "Why so serious?"

He shakes his head and walks to the window.

I tell him about my dream, how sorry I am that the kids have lost precious time with him. He doesn't respond. "You're acting weird," I say.

"Things have changed."

"Like what? You seeing someone else?"

"Yes," he turns and faces me. "I was lonely."

I drop to the rug, like a sparrow shot from a tree, lean back against the wall, draw my knees to my chest.

"I thought you weren't coming back," he says, sitting down in front of me.

"Does she know that you're married?"

"I told her we were separated. She wants us to get a place."

"When were you going to tell me?"

Silence. He picks at the shag.

"Do you want to live with her?"

"It was just a physical thing."

"Oh Sonny," I moan. "I never imagined that you'd do this."

"It just happened. I met her on vacation during Holy Week."

The same week I'd dreamed of him! Maybe the same night! He stares out the window.

"So you really like her?"

"I don't know. We were just starting out."

"Just starting out..." I repeat. Is this my husband? "I'm raising our kids and you're dating." My insides ache. "What am I going to tell them?" I sob.

"We don't have to tell them anything," he says, taking my hands.

"Why didn't you write and tell me?"

"I love you. Please. Just come back to Mexico."

I lie down on the carpet. More tears. Damn it. How can he have so much power over me? He's silent. Is it because he's ashamed of the affair, or because he doesn't know how to respond to my meltdown?

I agree to return to Mexico with the kids on two conditions: he cancels his trip to France and he never sees this woman again.

Back in Mexico I have mixed feelings about Sonny and doubts about myself. Why did he pursue a relationship with another woman? I'm not good enough? Smart enough? My mind spins, I don't eat. What do I want for my family? If I stay I'll need to redesign myself, readjust my ingrained beliefs of what marriage is supposed to be and relearn what love looks like.

To make matters worse, Sonny rented the little house on our property to Jorge, a friend of the errant woman.

Sonny hasn't been home in two nights. He says he has extra opera rehearsals. My imagination is out of control. I need a distraction, so I wander out to Jorge's house. He's bent over one of his clay sculptures, shaping a spear for the raised hand of a foot-high, green Poseidon, waist deep in churning waves. I take a chair next to him.

"Do you know where Sonny stays when he doesn't come home?" I ask him.

"No I don't," he says, without looking up. "Face the fact." He rolls a thin snake between both hands. "If Sonny loved you, he wouldn't have dated her. You should get out of this pathetic relationship while you're young enough to find someone else." He stops and stares at me. "Why did you come back and ruin it for them? They were so happy together." My head is going to explode. This is the "worse" of "for better or for worse." I promised to love through this, but how could I have known it would be so suffocating?

I can never go back to the orchestra. She attended all his concerts, a classical music groupie. My colleagues knew and no one told me; they're all as guilty as he is.

Then, one rainy day, a friend drops by with a book, a life preserver that keeps me afloat for a few months: The Monogamy Myth, by Peggy Vaughan. Finally, a balm for my brokenness. The book logically explains the reality of infidelity.

According to the author, we're taught, even in children's stories, that one day we'll marry and "live happily ever after." With a faithful husband. But it's unrealistic; this isn't how Nature works. Women come to expect what is biologically impossible: sexual fidelity.

It makes sense. Why do our parents and society intentionally set us up for disappointment? Santa, the tooth fairy, faithful men: all lies. It's comforting to know that I'm not alone. Thousands, if not millions, of women (possibly a few men), are working to make sense of the fairy tale at this very moment.

And yet, I can't believe my father or my brothers would break their promise, betray themselves, their own integrity. They just wouldn't.

For the next two years I fight to banish images of my husband with another woman. I have no reason to doubt Sonny's promise that he's faithful now, but his affair is an insurmountable shadow. Even though I drown myself in violin practice and caring for the kids, I'm miserable.

1995 TAMPICO TRAVESTY

The trust of the innocent is the liar's most useful tool.
- Stephen King

I awake to the smell of diesel and peer through a slit in the curtains at daybreak fog. The bus cruises along a two-lane, no-shoulder highway, passing lumbering trucks, modern day burros, heavy with overflowing crates of bright-red tomatoes. Six hours ago, around midnight, two buses of musicians, with spouses and children, suitcases and instruments left Mexico City to join a brand-new orchestra in Tampico.

For almost two years I've been working to keep my family together. I don't want my kids to suffer through a divorce; I've never seen a clean one. Sonny hopes a change of scenery might charge our marriage with new life, hopes to put the past behind us. His past.

Danny and I arrive mid-morning on the first bus, Sonny and Roxy a few hours later in our VW Bug, packed with double bass, household goods, and a TV. A modest hotel will be our home for a week, while we look for permanent housing. Rehearsals begin tomorrow.

In the afternoons, while I look for a house in the scorching heat, Sonny and the kids hang out at the beach with new-found musician friends. I find an unfurnished, three-bedroom and ask the owner if she'll wait for our first paycheck. We register Danny for fifth grade at a private school. Registration fees, books, and three uniforms (sports, every day and sweats) take a chunk of our savings. Roxy is homeschooled and Pete is at Scattergood Friends School in Iowa.

Weeks of rehearsals whiz by and no mention of checks. "The orchestra account is in dollars and the bank has frozen the account until the dollar stops fluctuating," the orchestra manager says. We're as nervous as horses tied in a burning barn. The director asks us to trust him: we'll be paid the night of the premier gala performance, a month to the day of our arrival.

Our spacious house is empty except for essentials: a card table with two plastic chairs and an ice chest, a queen-size sponge mattress in each room; a two-burner camp stove and sink in the kitchen. No refrigerator, no water heater, no mirrors.

Slava, a double bassist from Mexico City, lends 26,000 pesos to the orchestra director to pay the hotel bill, guaranteeing him the principal chair. Some say that Slava is KGB, keeping an eye on his comrades who fled Russia when the curtain fell in 1989. But we only know him as generous. He invites starving musicians to his house for three meals a day.

Two concerts are scheduled for the last weekend in the month, most musicians threatening to walk out if checks don't appear after the first.

Beethoven is surely smiling on our impeccable performance of his 9th Symphony and the director beams to deafening applause, but no mention is made of the promised cash. Newspaper reporters and television crews are on site. Not only do they record this historic event, but also interview disgusted musicians. Tonight, we realize that this concert was a sales pitch to potential patrons. There is no foundation, no bank account, no money. The barn has burned to the ground. We escaped, but we did it on our own.

El Mundo Tampico, Tamps. 12 de marzo de 1995

Miembros de la Orquesta Filarmónica Fueron Abandonados a su Suerte

MEMBERS OF THE PHILHARMONIC ORCHESTRA ABANDONED TO THEIR LUCK

The orchestra meets in the auditorium the following morning and the general manager, alone and defenseless, is ambushed on arrival.

"I have no job!" "My kids are going to lose the school year!" "We don't have money to get back to Mexico City!" "You're playing with our lives!"

Three violinists lunge at the manager and pin him to the floor. Fists fly. Shouting. More jump into the fray. "Do something!" "They'll kill him!" Sonny and a few others pull the assailants from the manager. Blood gushing, he runs from the auditorium.

News of the orchestra scam ripples through Tampico. Townspeople respond, flooding the trombonist's house with bags of food. We're all invited to take what we need. A group of citizens takes up a collection to buy bus tickets for those returning to Mexico City.

Once again, goodwill has triumphed.

1995

GOING BACK

Have enough courage to trust love one more time and always one more time. - Maya Angelou

It's been three months since we parted at the Texas border. In my head, Sonny's infidelity is a broken record, the needle stuck at my failure to "be good enough." I keep busy, pretend I'm happy, but can't nudge the needle from its groove. The only solution is to change records.

After I leave Roxy and Pete at boarding schools in Iowa and Pennsylvania, I call Sonny and tell him that Danny and I will live at my brother Henry's in Michigan, in the basement, a dungeon for the wounded, prisoners of love.

I need to decide what to do with the rest of my life. Henry suggests I learn a new career: train to become a paramedic or real estate agent. "Take as long as you need," he says. I'll never abandon my violin.

I register Danny at the overcrowded junior high school. His first day he can't figure out how to open his locker or why he needs brand name sneakers.

Something stirs deep, a force trumping reason, an unbearable sorrow for the death of who I thought I was. I'd committed to love, "for better or worse." But now, it seems too formidable a task.

Sonny writes that he's devastated, we are his family, he loves me. "Please reconsider."

If I were to meet him tomorrow, for the first time, I'd hop on the back of his motorcycle in a second. He'd seduce me with talk about his quest for spiritual enlightenment, his happy-go-lucky, carefree manner, and dimples to die for. Add a night of passion and I'd be under his spell forever.

As one day blurs into the next, the center of my being swells with sorrow unimaginable.

It's day four. I'm not eating; delirium is setting in, and lurid scenes of Sonny with his lover drift through my head. I regret that my family is broken, scattered like shards of a priceless broken goblet.

Nights are endless tunnels of confusion. I don't sleep. Day breaks with life lines: cooing babies and coffee brewing in the kitchen above.

My soul is withering, shutting down. I'm desperate and call Mexico.

"I'm dying," I say. "I don't know what to do."

"Come back," Sonny says. "I'm here for you."

We take it one painful day at a time. Sonny brings me coffee in bed, polishes my violin, and massages my feet. I need time. I will survive. It's an opportunity to test my promise to love unconditionally, to honor my commitment to this divine sacred work.

1997

SERENDIPITY

The best way to find yourself is to lose yourself in the service of others. - Mahatma Gandhi

In 1996, without a word, my sister Christie's husband walks out on her and their three young boys, 8, 10 and 14 years old. Reality splintered, grief paralyzes even the most basic of her daily routines.

She needs help but lives in Falls Church, Virginia, 2,500 miles away. This will mean a lot of changes for us: Sonny will need to quit his job in the Mexico City orchestra, Danny will change schools again, and we'll need to find work. But Christie needs a lifeline or she's going down, dragging her boys with her. "This is the right thing to do," I tell Sonny. "It will work out."

We rent our house and head north. Christie offers Sonny and me her bedroom, the master suite on the lower level, complete with a wooden deck and hot tub. She and the boys share three rooms on the second floor.

It's September, a few weeks into the school year. I

know chances for a teaching position are slim, so I sign up as a substitute teacher.

At home we comfort tender souls with hot meals and midnight chats. Sonny is a constant, loving presence for the boys. He listens. He doesn't always nurture them the way I think he should, but he is there for them, his way just as valid.

I even walk Bear, the beloved family mutt, neglected now, a casualty of the strangling sorrow consuming us all. One day, as Bear pulls me through the neighborhood, I notice an old elementary school with Leis Instructional Center, Fairfax County Public Schools in bold letters. Next door, on a sign outside a house identical to my sister's, I read Music Department. I can't believe my luck. This is the tenth largest school district in the United States with 198 schools and centers, and music teacher contracting is four blocks away! I run the dog home and I'm back in flash.

The worst thing they can say is no, I think, as I climb the steps and knock.

A secretary shows me into the converted living room, filing cabinets and a large desk against the back wall, violin and cello cases stacked in piles around the room. "Sorry it's such a mess, " she says. "This arrangement is temporary until they give us real offices."

"Do you know if they need an orchestra teacher?" I ask and hold my breath.

"What did you say?" a lady says, her head poking from the adjacent bedroom-office.

"Are there any openings for orchestra or music teachers?"

"You've just dropped from heaven," she says,

motioning me into her office. "We manage sixty string teachers in the county and one just quit yesterday."

Sonny finds a job at a tree-trimming business. Bud is the owner and sole employee. He's blond, sunburned and built like a wrestler.

One day, I come home to a police car parked at the curb. A policeman approaches as I get out.

"Do you own a black Dodge van?" he says.

"I do, but my husband has it out on a job."

"What kind of job would that be? They spotted your van at the scene of a $200,000 dollar robbery over in Alexandria. Thought you might be gypsies."

After I tell the policeman that I teach high school orchestra and my husband trims trees, he takes his hand off his holstered gun. "I think you've got the wrong person," I say.

"It looks that way," he says. "Sorry we bothered you."

1998

ACAPULCO

A truthful enemy is better than a deceitful friend.
- Matshona Dhliwayo

It's summer, 1998 when Señor Rojas (Mr. Reds) calls asking Sonny and me if we'd like to be part of a new orchestra project in Acapulco. Our marriage has miraculously improved through caring for my sister and her boys. We see what happens to little lives when promises are shattered, and how our commitment has helped them to heal. Now, after two years, it's time to go. Sonny and I miss Mexico and here's our ticket back: performing in an orchestra at a famous beach town.

Acapulco is a tourist hub. Even the public busses pulsate disco music, fluorescent strobe lights flashing inside and out. But we don't feel like partying. Salty humidity drains us of energy, and our clothes, wet with perspiration, cling to our skin.

Tropi-chico, Tropic Guy, a cellist friend we know from freelance work, invites us to Dora, his wife's birthday celebration. I've never met Dora, concertmistress of the Acapulco Symphony, but destiny is persistent. She's my age and immigrated from Poland the same year I came to Mexico. After a few weeks, she's teaching me Polish and inviting me over to swim in her pool.

Professionals from Mexico City aren't interested in this rickety orchestra venture; there are no contracts and salaries are paid in cash. So, the director flies to Armenia to recruit more than half the orchestra. They're a sly lot. In less than a year they speak Spanish and become Mexican citizens, something I've wanted to do for over thirty years. I refuse to pay the bribes!

We find a seventh-floor apartment with no elevator but a fantastic view of the convention center and palm-dotted golf course. Beyond that the neon-lit hotel strip blinks pink and orange, bordering the ink black shadow of the Pacific Ocean. We leave the floor-to-ceiling windows open all night and luscious winds blow relief.

At the first rehearsal, the director greets us warmly from the podium.

I first met the Maestro in 1977 at the *Conservatorio Nacional de Música* in Mexico City, where I studied violin. Sporting a hooked nose and bulging eyes, my classmates nicknamed him "Paganini." Portrait drawings of the time proved he was indeed a doppelganger of the violin virtuoso.

Paganini was an outcast. He was the last one chosen for quartet practice; there was never room in the car for him when we'd head out to play a midnight serenade; and we cringed at his jokes and blatant brown-nosing of teachers.

I'd lost touch with Paganini and now, twenty years later, here we are, amazed that he has his own orchestra.

He hasn't changed much except for round-shoulders, grey hair, and a few wrinkles. My stand partner whispers that his new nickname is "Mr. Burns," from the cartoon The Simpsons. He now resembles, in countenance as well as character, the owner of the nuclear power plant where Homer Simpson works.

Paganini introduces Sonny and me as friends from his youth, rambling on about intimate friendships, his accordion solos with the orchestra, and how his colleagues marveled at his violin prowess.

"Laurie and Sonny can even vouch for me. I was a virtuoso. That's why they baptized me Paganini."

I am dumbfounded. He was, in fact, an average musician, but with this accolade burning in his brain, he rose to direct his own symphony orchestra!

We don't just play classical music in the Acapulco Symphony. Once we accompany Enrique Iglesias, the son of the singer, Julio.

The manager wants twenty-five violinists at center stage on a five-stepped bleacher. The performance is all pre-recorded. We move our bows up and down, pretending to play. There aren't enough authentic violinists available, so some trombones, a clarinet, and the entire percussion section is drafted. After a five-minute lesson on how to hold a bow and violin, they're good to go.

I'm in the cafeteria when Enrique arrives, knocking over chairs and yelling at his crew.

Two "guitarists" and a "bassist," dressed in ripped jeans and tight t-shirts, their bleached hair combed and sprayed up in points, approach a stand with eight guitars.

They're painted bright red, orange and blue. They don't have strings.

"I want the yellow one," spiked blond hair says. "It goes good with my pants."

They choose their instruments like crayons from a box. They won't be playing either, we're all pretending. Everything is prerecorded; the whole concert is a hoax.

The Miss Mexico Pageant was last night, so there's a runway and Enrique loves the idea of walking into his audience, pressed up against the stage. During one song, he bends over, plucks a toddler from her mother's arms, props her on his hip and croons.

Professionals are of another caliber, classy and polished. One evening, I enter the convention hall through a side door and notice a grey-haired man in front of me, a high-heeled, well-dressed lady at his side. The man covers one side of his face with a fist holding his jacket slung over his shoulder, smooth as a random onlooker. It's Placido Domingo. He's the soloist and he brings his own conductor to direct a concert of popular pieces. In spite of false starts and intonation problems in the woodwinds, the maestro is always encouraging and praises the orchestra.

This concert is special: admissions fees will be used to rebuild houses in Acapulco, damaged by Hurricane Paulina in 1997.

We always know which countries in the world are suffering by the new faces that pop up in the orchestras: Guatemalans and Salvadorans flooded the State of Mexico Symphony in the seventies; Russians and Poles in the eighties; and now it's the Armenians, Georgians and others from the Former Soviet Union.

The pay is bad, and there's little work, they say. But they love the Motherland.

"I'm proud of being Armenian," violinist Ruben says. "Unlike you sad Americans, we have our own culture and customs."

"What are you talking about?" I say. "You've never even been to the United States."

"It's like Russia used to be," he says. "It has a lot of different countries within its borders, but soon it's going to have to give them their independence. In California there are twenty million Armenians. Friends there are already talking independence," he says.

"The kids of different nationalities, including Armenians, who are born in the United States will adopt the culture and customs of America, whether you like it or not," I say.

Our kids come to Acapulco over Christmas vacation. One day, they drive out to Playa Diamante (Diamond Beach), outside the protected bay area and, unknown to me, infamous for undertow drownings.

Just back from rehearsal, the phone rings. "Do you have an extra key for the car?" Pete asks, voice tense. "We lost it in the sand."

"We don't, but maybe we can find it," I say. "Where are you?"

A friend drives Sonny and me out to the beach. Usually boisterous Pete and Danny meet us in the parking lot, silent as pallbearers. We retrace their steps and rake the sand in scorching noonday sun, but no keys. "It's not a big deal," I say.

"We're not going to find them," Pete says finally, scanning the horizon. "They're out there. Danny was swimming alone, and I got distracted," he swallows.

"Because you were talking to some girls," Danny says.

Pete ignores him. "Those guys in the red t-shirts swam out to save him."

"I couldn't beat the tide," Danny says. "But I remembered what you said, Mom, to stay calm. I looked out and saw land." He motions to a jetty two miles out to sea.

He never would have made it.

"A wave took my shoes with the keys and my money. We didn't want to tell you Danny almost drowned, but now these guys want money," Pete says, nodding at the two young, tanned locals with short dreadlocks. The self-appointed lifeguards, twenty feet away, heads down, arms crossed, kick shells in the sand. "They prey on peoples' misfortune."

"There should be paid lifeguards on these beaches," I say. "But it's not a priority to take care of their tourists."

I thank the lifeguards with enough cash to feed them and their families for a month. A locksmith makes us a new key. Cheap lessons, I think.

Dora and I form a quintet to play for events and concerts. As concertmistress of the orchestra, she plays impeccable solos; I'm so lucky to play with one of the best. We call ourselves *Camerata de Oro* (Golden Chamber Orchestra). It's easy to remember and it says it all: we sparkle. Soon, we're booked every Saturday, the day the maestro insists on village concerts. He hires and fires musicians like a third world dictator, programming for concerts and rehearsals top secret until the last minute. He learns, from planted musician-spies, that *Camerata de Oro* has all the extra work in town, reason enough to be banished.

In May, Sonny and I ask for a week off to attend Roxy's graduation from George School, in the US. The manager agrees to let us go as long as we send substitutes. Marilu and Sam promise to cover for us, so we fly off, worry-free, to celebrate this milestone.

The day after we return, the orchestra manager calls. "The Maestro says not to bother coming in to work. You missed all last week and no substitutes showed up."

"I gave you their names and phone numbers," I say. "You know them."

SONNY, DORA, BARBARA, LAURIE

"You're fired," he says, and hangs up.

I call Marilu. "The manager said they wouldn't need us," she says.

We have no money and the kids are coming home for summer vacation. At least we have our homestead in Huitzilac.

Sonny doesn't sleep at night and shuffles around like a zombie during the day. I post an ad on the Cuernavaca Community web site: AVAILABLE TO TUNE YOUR PIANO FOR THE NEXT TWO WEEKS ONLY. I'm swamped with work. Then, I make new business cards for *Camerata de Oro*, call every banquet service, garden, wedding planner, band, and restaurant. I advertise: TWENTY YEARS OF EXPERIENCE; PUNCTUAL, CLASSY, AND NO RECORDED MUSIC. In a month's time we're back in the game, earning double what we'd made in Acapulco. Tragedy turned blessing.

CAMERATA DE ORO – WEDDING ON THE BEACH

1998

AUNTIE LAURIE´S FINISHING SCHOOL

Life is a great big canvas, and you should throw all the
paint you can on it. - Danny Kaye

At the Mexico City Airport arrival gate it's easy to
recognize my fifteen-year-old nephew, Worthington. His
waist-long, blond hair, parted down the middle, covers
most of his face, just a nose poking out.

For weeks he doesn't speak to anyone unless he needs
something, and spends hours alone in his room making
tiny, detailed clay figures. He and his twin sisters were
home-schooled by my sister in Pennsylvania all their lives.
Maybe he just doesn't know how to connect.

Friends stop over frequently, and Worthington is always
greeted with a flurry of hugs, kisses and questions: *¿Cómo*
te llamas? What's your name? *¿De dónde eres?* Where
are you from?   He struggles to answer, beaming when
they nod in response.

With caution I try to polish behaviors and attitudes, and Worthington seems receptive. "It may not be of any interest to you now," I say, "maybe even file this for another occasion, but most people, especially girls, think it's disgusting if you lick your fingers when you're done eating, if you don't shower, if you put your feet on the table..."

A few weeks later, Worthington wants to explore Cuernavaca, a half-hour down the hill.

"I can drop you off, but can't pick you up," I say. "I'm busy this afternoon."

"I have to get back by myself?"

"It's easy. Get off the bus when you see the chicken farm, and head down the dirt road."

I give him the bus fare and drop him off downtown. "Look for the bus that says Huitzilac when you're ready to come home."

He narrows his eyes, shakes his head, and slams the door.

When I arrive later that evening Worthington is sitting at the table, arms crossed, chin up.

"I did it. By myself."

This is the first triumph of many: Next, he meets Lily, who teaches him Spanish while they make *enchiladas* and he draws her posing in the garden. He finds a job teaching English at a language school and discovers a Chinese couple selling trinkets downtown who teach him some Chinese. Finally, he has his first taste of the theater, playing the young Scrooge in the English-speaking community play, A Christmas Carol.

Having outgrown his long, golden locks, Worthington

crops and bleaches his hair white and dons a mid-calf, maroon, suede coat. "What do you think of my new look?" he says.

"Fabulous," I say.

Then, one day, Worthington asks if he can go with some friends to a remote, hippy-infested beach on the Pacific.

"No way, it's too dangerous," I say, as my brain swarms with gun-slinging bandidos, backpacking pot smokers, and a bobbing Worthington, dragged out to sea.

He listens in silence, arms akimbo, digging the dirt with the toe of his sandal. "OK," he nods, and walks off.

The next morning he's gone, off recklessly testing his new-plumaged wings, soaring by now.

I call my sister. "Worthington's gone to the beach," I say. "He disobeyed. If something happens, we're responsible. We can't take care of him anymore."

The day after he returns from his week of debauchery, Sonny and I drive Worthington to the airport. My heart flutters as he hugs us and then turns to strut through airport security, chin high.

Word spreads about Worthington's awakening and soon a steady stream of nieces and nephews arrive to enroll in what becomes known as Auntie Laurie's Finishing School, even though Sonny works his magic in subtle ways, planting pine trees with them along the fence, baking whole wheat bread, and guiding our impressionable subjects in mindful yoga and meditation.

2002

BEHIND THE SCENES

The road to success is always under construction.
- Lily Tomlin

My soul soars in ethereal ecstasy when I perform but, before that's possible, there's a lot of behind-the-scenes drudgery. Organizing repertoire, equipment and transportation is easy compared to dealing with musicians, who make my life a soap-opera nightmare. Prima donnas abound, their emotional closets bursting with traumatic childhoods and trampled egos. For example, Sonny hates taking orders from a woman. If I'm lucky, he gets dressed and loads his bass in the car on time. But those are mere foothills compared to the Mt. Everest of our quartet business: finances. Hike after grueling hike towards the top, with no financial map, I lose my way, don't insist on prepayment, run out of provisions, and forget my equipment.

Alberto, the owner of a garden venue and an event

coordinator, hires us to play for a wedding. I believe him when he says he'll pay us at the church.

Alberto is nowhere when the mass begins in the 16th century stone cathedral in downtown Cuernavaca. Our quartet sits in half-circle formation next to the gold-plated altar, facing the congregation. During communion I glare at the twelve-foot wooden front doors, willing Alberto to appear. At the end of the service, heat rises from my chest as I wrap my violin in flannel and tuck it away. I have no money to pay my colleagues! Suddenly, Alberto is at my elbow, shoving a white envelope towards me. "Take it," he pants. "I've got to get back to the reception."

I can't count money at the altar. Outside, I tear open the envelope. One bill looks like it fell out of a Monopoly game. My heart drops. I know Alberto is busy with his event, so I wait until the next day to call.

"Impossible," he says. "There's nothing we can do about it now. We have to wait until the bride and groom return from their honeymoon."

"But you're the one who paid me," I say.

A few months later, Alberto calls for another wedding.

"You need to pay the 500 pesos first," I say. And he does.

But I still don't learn and it gets worse. Lizzi, a wedding planner, hires us and promises to pay us before the wedding starts. We arrive extra early.

"After the ceremony," she says, rushing by with arms full of flowers. "The groom hasn't paid me. This is not a good time to bother him."

A week later, Lizzi claims she still doesn't have the payment.

"Give me the groom's number," I say. "I'll call."

"That's impossible," she says. "That would be a breach of confidentiality."

"I played for free," I say. "And I had to pay the others."

"Just give me some time. My brother died last week, my boyfriend dumped me, and I'm out of work."

I feel bad for her. She's basically just fallen off the mountain. Maybe pushed by some angry musicians. But a few months later she wants us for another wedding. She's straggling back up.

"You still owe us," I say.

"Play for this one and I'll pay you for both," she says.

I turn her down. I have a better chance of surviving without her.

But then I'm tricked again. This couple is in their seventies and have lived together for thirty years. I meet with them at their Spanish colonial home, in their magenta-flaming bougainvillea garden, next to an Olympic size swimming pool. We'll play during the ceremony and dinner, three hours total, in the gingerbread-trimmed gazebo between twenty-foot palm trees.

They sign the contract and give me half our fee, promising the rest before the event. A doctor should be good for his word, especially one living in this affluence.

We're the first to arrive and I remind the groom of our deal. *"Ahorita,"* in a second, he says.

"I'm sorry," the doctor says when we finish. "My wife has your money. She wasn't feeling well and has retired for the evening. Call my secretary next week."

I call the following week, and the next, reminding the secretary of the doctor's promise.

"This Friday," she says. But two months of Fridays pass and nothing. Then, one day in January, the truth:

"The doctor's wife died of cancer on Christmas Eve," she says. "They were married for only a month. He has a lot of debts from the funeral."

I tell Judith, our pianist, about the doctor's debt and his bride's death. "I can't call anymore."

"You have to get paid," she says. "It's terrible that the doctor lost his wife, but that's not your problem. He made a deal with you."

After four months, no rescue team in sight, hope long gone, the secretary calls. The money is in our account.

"The balance must be paid a week before the event," I say over the phone to another bride seeking price quotes.

"We're nervous you might not come," bride Marcela says. "Can you let us pay on the day?" I fall for it. On my face. In gravel.

The minute we arrive, I remind Marcela of our deal, as she rustles by in picture-taking frenzy in her white taffeta gown. *"Ahorita,"* she says, and brushes me away.

In casual, pre-nuptial chatter I mention my predicament to the priest, who is setting up the altar with chalice and wafers. "Better be careful with them," he says. "I had to chisel my fee out of them."

The bridesmaids are lined up to enter the aisle, the groom and his mother in the lead. She motions for us to play the Bridal March. I shake my head. Again she motions. She's flailing now. I walk back and whisper that she hasn't paid yet.

She rolls her eyes and shakes her head, tsk tsk, then motions to a guest in the back row. "Juanita, please, collect the 2,000 pesos we owe this woman, so she'll play."

Women rummage in purses, men take out billfolds and the missing payment appears.

I'm still struggling up the mountain of business finances, now almost to the top. It helps to pretend I'm someone else when I discuss fees and deadlines. And I cancel events of clients not willing to invest in the expedition a week before.

2002

A QUARTET OF CONCERTS

The nature of reality is this: it is hidden, it is hidden, and it is hidden. - Rumi

My neighbor, Franco, calls late one night in August 2002. He and his wife are in their forties and still go by the nickname *Los Duendes*, The Elves. She dresses in ankle-length hippie skirts, beads, finger and toe rings, he in long tunics and leather sandals, both with hair to their waists, peace-and-love babble. They were reared in wealthy families. Pseudo elves.

He wants to know if I can play violin for a concert in the National Auditorium.

"The radio station EXA is hosting a huge rock concert with all the famous groups in Mexico," Franco says. "One rehearsal and two concerts, 1,000 pesos ($100 US) per service."

"You want me to play violin with your rock group?"

"Not exactly with my group."

"I don't improvise. If you have music, I'll do it."

"No, man, you can play whatever you want. We'll be rockin' out, and over top you wail on your violin. And think symphony garb: long-dress formal. And heels."

I convince 19-year-old Danny to tag along. "It'll be fun to see all the big-name bands."

We're on time for the 3:00 o'clock rehearsal, but the stage is a mess of tangled cables. Seven audio technicians in black T-shirts stumble around on stage hooking one cable after another into 10-foot crackling speakers. Hours tick by. The concert is tomorrow!

Franco, The Elf, points to four columns sprouting out of the auditorium halfway back from the stage, 25 feet apart. "I'll be drummin' it up on that one, sax'll be jammin' on second, electric guitar there, and that one's yours!" he says.

Almost midnight, the audio nightmare unresolved, Danny and I leave for home. With no rehearsal, I'm worried. We, the "Musicians of the Four Pillars," are the opening act.

The next day the audio issues are resolved, cables invisible. People filter in and take seats, the auditorium buzzing to capacity. A few seconds before the show starts, the venue goes black and two young stagehands lift me onto the column, a real struggle in heels and a fan blowing my long white chiffon dress. A commercial about EXA radio station bursts from a huge screen above the stage and the audience erupts into a frenzy of chanting and clapping. Suddenly, a spotlight, and Franco appears in a fog, long hair bobbing, a drum thrashing, crazed phantom.

Oh crap! That light's coming my way!

At one-minute intervals the other musicians are spotted until the final light is on me. I break into a Vivaldi violin concerto, my violin soaring above the throbbing crowd and pulsating rock accompaniment. The crowd is standing now, screaming, arms swaying in the air. Someone turns on a fog machine at the base of my column and I'm blinded by acrid smoke. I can't breathe. Coughing, I drop into two pairs of outstretched arms, my violin and bow waving in the air, as if in surrender to rock music. Without missing a beat, I'm whisked out a side door to fresh air.

Months later The Elf calls. "You were great," he says. "You can pick up your 2,000 pesos."

"A rehearsal is the same amount as a concert, even if we didn't rehearse," I say. "It should be three."

Next time, I'll clarify working conditions.

The event that shaves years off my life takes place one day after my 50th birthday, a splendid celebration, attended by family and friends, including my *"Comadre"* Carmen, and her Polish boyfriend, Jan. I've hired them both to play violin with Sonny (on double bass) and me (on piano) for a concert the following day.

On her arrival, Carmen whispers that Jan hasn't had a drink in six months.

I hope he stays off the bottle for good, for Carmen's sake.

The alcohol-saturated ambiance is too tempting for Jan and by the end of the night Carmen and a few friends have to carry him to their car.

"We have a concert at Peña de Bernal tomorrow, 7:30 sharp," I remind her, as she closes the door.

"I know where it is. Tomorrow Jan should be fine. Don't worry."

The place is enchanting. A stage sits at the foot of the

third-tallest monolith in the world, towering over 1,000 feet above us. Little village streets wind up around the tourist attraction, and we've got time to window gaze.

It's 7:30 and Carmen and Jan are nowhere. My *comadre* is never late. Where are they? At 8:00, my stomach is churning. It's a full house and the audience begins their clap-clap-claps of impatience. At 8:20 I call again, and Carmen finally answers.

"Laurie, we've been here since seven, but Jan is cussing drunk. He hasn't stopped since your party. He's furious that you tricked us. You didn't tell him that this place was so far."

"Can he play?" I ask

"Most drunks can perform once you get them in the chair," she says.

"Let's do it then."

I thank the audience for their patience, "I'm so very sorry for the delay." Then I put music on stands, as Sonny helps Jan to his seat and hands him his violin. We begin with an easy piece. Jan plays well, despite his drunkenness but now, an invisible cohort: the wind, whipping our clothes-pin-tethered music, threatening to toss music stands into the audience. After the applause dies down, Jan begins an alcohol-inspired soliloquy.

"We're so grateful that you appreciate us," he says. "Hours and hours we prepare for you, in solitary confinement, our reward - your applause. We thank you."

The audience applauds again, louder now, and gasps as he tilts forward, snapping back upright just before falling.

Finally, intermission! But no relief. The universe deals another cruel card: they're serving wine in our honor - all the wine we can drink in half an hour. Jan's eyes light up and he grabs two goblets from the tray of a passing, white-gloved waiter. "One's for my girlfriend," he winks.

The concert is doomed. I feel faint and run to find a bathroom where, alone in my misery, I vomit. There's no electricity and no water to flush my mess. The wine-induced chatter and tenuous light filter down through dirty windows where I sit.

Drying my eyes, I find Sonny sampling and toasting.

"I'm really sick," I say.

"Oh yeah, this place is known for its powerful energy force," he says. "Any feelings you have are going to be intensified. I'm feeling really good right now!"

As usual, he's unconcerned that I'm dying or that Jan is guzzling. To make matters even worse, the organizers of the concert give us each a bottle of wine as a souvenir. We're in wine country after all, and they're proud of it.

The audience demands an encore as we take our final bow. "La Cucaracha!" Jan says, dropping down into his seat. And so we end this nightmare.

Unloading the car at home, I realize that our wine bottles are missing. I call Carmen to thank her for her support; the event could easily have ended our friendship.

She confirms that Jan has our bottles.

Most concerts aren't so chaotic but performing for young audiences has unique challenges. Loyola University in Cuernavaca hires my quintet to perform Mexican Fantasy at the closing ceremony of their Cultural Week. I've arranged a program of Mexican songs for three violins, piano, bass and drum set and introduce each number with a fun fact, like:

"Did you know that *"Bésame"* and *"Perfidia,"* both

written by Mexican composers, were the two most popular pieces among American troops during the Second World War?"

The venue is in Chapultepec Park, a tin roof protecting us from the sun, plastic white chairs set up for the public. About a hundred high-school-aged, uniformed kids regard us with as much enthusiasm as a history exam.

During the first selection a girl in the second row, fingers dancing wildly on a cell phone, catches my eye. My mind races as we bow to applause: How can I end this torture? What pieces should I cut?

I scan the audience: Seven kids sit in a circle, laughing and talking; some writing, others reading. Teachers stand in the back, chatting. But it's the kid with the earphones, listening to his iPod that snaps my patience. Amid shocked, questioning glances from the violinists, I rip the microphone from the stand, unconcerned with protocol or who I might offend.

"This is a concert," I say. "By the looks of it, most of you have never attended a cultural event in your lives. (I'm straining to be gentle). We're offering you a gift from our hearts to yours, but to receive this treasure you need to put away your cell phones and video games; close your books, your notepads, and your mouths. Music, theater, poetry, everything we call "art" is nourishment for your souls, you might even experience something mystical. But we need quiet for the magic to work."

Silence. We wait. Then, the kids in the circle straighten their chairs, all the electrical gadgets, books, and pencils disappear. As soon as the rustling stops, we begin again, and when it's over, deafening applause.

As we pack up, I notice, from the corner of my eye, the

director of the school approaching. Here it comes. I insulted her students!

"Your little speech was wonderful!" the director says, grabbing my hand. "They had no idea how to behave at a concert. And that part about being quiet to connect to the divine. That was brilliant!"

The musical extravaganza, *El Tepozteco*, written and directed by Federico Alvarez del Toro, is about the complicated legend of Tepozteco. His mother is impregnated by the wind, and then she and his human father abandon Tepozteco on an ant hill. The ants feed him morsels of food and stash him in a maguey plant, which drips sweet nectar into his mouth. An older couple find and adopt him, and Tepozteco, a superior warrior, later becomes king of Tepoztlán.

Our friend, Federico, plans an elaborate musical reenactment of these events to honor Tepozteco. Rehearsals are in Tepoztlan's city auditorium, but the concert venue is down the road, near Santo Domingo, on a large swath of barren land surrounded by mountains.

The string section is mostly Russian, and by the time Sonny and I arrive at the rehearsal, the brass and woodwinds are buzzing-angry about them. Unlike the rest of the orchestra, they've been invited to stay at a luxury hotel in town, and can sign for anything they want, even, according to them, massages and bottles of whisky. Worse, the Russians openly mock and scorn the conductor and the piece, El Tepozteco: "What kind of a joke is this?" "We repeat the same measure sixty-four times!" "It's a vacuum of creativity!"

Two hours before curtain time, carpenters are still

hammering away on the rock-concert-size stage. The white plastic chairs for the audience sit in two sections with an aisle down the center. Along the outside large piles of bonfire wood are stacked at ten-feet intervals, to be lit at sun-down, crackling warmth and color to Federico's music. Actors and dancers are warming up voices and muscles. A famous Mexican pre-Hispanic musician blows his conch shell, shakes his rain sticks, and taps his teponaxtli, a ceremonial drum made from a hollowed-out log.

The concert, as often happens, begins over an hour late, and when Federico appears in his flowing white pants, a shirt with long chiffon wings, and long strings of shells around his neck, the Russians scoff and snicker.

Surely, they´ve never produced something of this magnitude.

The house is overflowing, the orchestra crisp, the actors on cue, but then the wind picks up. We musicians are on a stage in front of and below the actors. Three indigenous men carry copal incense burners as an offering to El Tepozteco. A gust of wind blows smoke and scatters lit coals over the orchestra. The trombone section runs for cover. Ten clothespins hold our music, but strong gusts whip sheets away every time we unpin to turn the page. Suddenly, like Dorothy's house, music stands fly into the air, dropping somewhere into the audience. A few dark shadows place the twisted metal on the podium at Federico's feet, and quickly return to their seats. The wind tugs and rattles the giant tarp above us, until screws and bolts rain down, a piece of metal chipping the belly of Cornelius's cello. The Russians are ready to run, but Federico refuses to stop conducting.

"Don't get up," he says.

"We're leaving," the concertmaster yells. "The whole stage is falling!"

"We finish the piece!" Federico shouts, without missing a beat. *"No pasa nada!"*

Every few measures, I spot another musician scurrying off the stage.

"It seems like El Tepozteco didn't like the concert we played in his honor," I say to Sonny, as we walk past the dying embers of the bonfires, the wind a gentle breeze.

"Of course he did!" he says. "He let us finish the piece, didn't he? He loved it."

2007

VIOLIN FOR SALE

The end justifies the means. - Niccoló Machiavelli

Sonny and I are visiting Houston and I'm looking for
violins to take back to my youth orchestra in Huitzilac.
On the way out of the supermarket I grab a free magazine
that advertises used goods for sale. The ads aren't listed in
any kind of order, so it takes me a while, but finally I see
it: Student Violin for Sale, also cello. Outside the store's
automatic doors I find a public phone and call the number.
An older man, with a southern accent, answers and gives
us directions to his neighborhood.

   Dark grey houses from the 1950s line both sides of the
street, with dusty front yards enclosed by four-foot-high
chain link fences. We let ourselves in through the
unlocked gate and knock on the weather-beaten door. A
man peeks through a small window and then opens and
invites us in. The living room is sparsely furnished with
only a few wooden, straight-backed chairs, and lacks even
the most minimal decoration. The absence of books on the

184

built-in bookshelves also surprises me, but I say nothing.

"My father was a music teacher in the western part of the state," he says. "He died a few months ago and left me with all his instruments."

"That must be difficult."

"I'm not a musician so I'm trying to sell them. What would you like to see, the violin or the cello?"

"Can we see the violin?"

He disappears down the hallway and brings back a brand-new student model. It's $100.

"Can we see the cello?"

"You can have the cello for $100 too," he says, showing us a shiny, brand-new model.

Sonny and I look at each other. Something's not right.

"We'll take both," I say. "We have a youth orchestra in Mexico, so we need instruments."

"Would ya like to see a viola or a double bass?"

For sure something's up. First, it's unheard of that a music teacher's son doesn't play an instrument. But even more amazing, these are brand new instruments; never been touched.

When the man leaves the room to fetch the viola and double bass, I quietly follow him down the hall and peek into the dining area. A whole wall of the room is missing, a tractor trailer backed up into the hole. The man is scrounging around deep inside the instrument-gorged truck. I scurry back to the living room.

We buy three violins, a viola, a cello and a double bass for only $600. Back in the car I tell Sonny about the missing wall. "We've probably just bought stolen goods," I say. "What should we do?"

"These instruments are for a good cause," Sonny says.

"They're tools to improve kids' lives."

A few weeks after returning to Mexico, our friend Marcos invites us to dinner. On his quaint, candlelit patio the conversation is lighthearted until it turns to Monica Veerkamp. Her family owns the largest and oldest music store in downtown Mexico City.

"One of the trailers full of musical instruments for the store was hijacked coming down from the United States. They lost everything."

We explain our adventure in Houston. Could the two incidents be related?

"It would be too much of a coincidence," Marcos says. "It'd be better if we just didn't say anything." And there we let it go. Supposedly.

But some nights I'm nudged awake, tossing and turning. What should we have done?

"You worry too much," Sonny says. "We can only go forward. No turning back now."

We'll never know if the instruments we bought are the same ones hijacked on a lonely stretch of desert highway. The only thing I can say for sure is that kids are flourishing in the orchestra, there's nothing that seals a relationship like partnering in crime and I have sacrificed long-held principals. Black and white has vanished.

2004

DON PABLO, SHAMAN

Set wide the window. Let me drink the day.
- Edith Wharton

We're returning home from visiting a friend in Tepoztlán,
a *Pueblo Mágico* (magic village), a half-hour drive from
our house, when the first domino topples in a series of
incredible events.

"I think this is his house," Sonny says, stopping in front
of a five-foot-high, sloppily mounted bamboo gate. "Let's
see if he's home." Classic Sonny: thirty-five years hanging
out, and I still haven't met all his friends! He can pull
surprises out of nowhere. This guy is still so much fun to
be around.

Peering over the gate, fifty feet beyond knee-high
weeds and a tangle of amate trees, we spy a Spanish
colonial-style house with a red-tiled roof. After Sonny
yells Don Pablo's name a few times, a figure emerges from
the house. I hold my breath as the man approaches, but a
wide smile proves he's the person we're looking for. Don
Pablo is dressed in white, loose-fitting peasant garb,
sandals, and a broad-brimmed hat. He hugs Sonny, shakes

my hand and leads us to the terrace, where we settle into rustic leather chairs. As they reminisce, I learn that Don Pablo had been John Cook's gardener for many years. Supposedly, John was a descendant of the famous explorer Captain James Cook and a good friend of Ingrid, Sonny's mom.

"John and my mom had set the date for their wedding." Sonny says. "I don't know what happened, but she called it off."

"I don't know either," says Don Pablo. "When John died thirty years ago, I inherited this house. Would you like to see his coffin?"

See his coffin? Is he still in it?

"Where is it?" Sonny asks, unruffled.

"It's back there, in the bungalow." Don Pablo points to an overgrown path. Bushes and vines partially hide a structure 30 feet from where we sit.

"Why is the coffin there?" I say.

"When John died, we buried him in my father's plot. Years passed and then my father died, and we needed the grave. So, we dug John up, took out what was left of him, wrapped him in a burlap bag, and put him deep in the hole. Then, over John's bones, we buried my father in his own coffin. John's coffin is now on display. Come, I'll show you."

It's getting dark. Twisted trees cast shadows across our path and thorns of wild blackberry bushes catch on our clothes as we walk.

"I must have forgotten the key," Don Pablo says when we arrive at the peeling dirty white door. "I'll be right back."

"Sonny, this is just too weird," I say.

188

"It's fine. We'll hurt his feelings if we leave now. Let's just see what he's got in there."

Stepping inside, my eyes fail me for a few seconds as they adjust to the darkness. Then I see it: the coffin standing on end in the center of the room. It's lined in dark-purple satin and shelved with mirrors wielding animal and human skulls.

"Are they real?" I ask.

"Of course they are," Don Pablo says proudly, hastily lighting a few candles on the floor.

Around the foot of the coffin are several vases of dead flowers, burnt candles in red glasses, and a few black-and-white pictures of John. Don Pablo dusts the pictures, peering at each as if trying to bring his old friend back to life.

I've seen enough, and suggest we return to the terrace, where Don Pablo invites us to a tea of Valerian. The conversation then takes an interesting turn.

"Did you know that Don Pablo is a shaman?" Sonny asks. "He even reads cards."

"I used to have lots of clients who'd come regularly, but they're all gone now," he says, as he looks over to where the cards sit on the sideboard.

"I've never had my cards read," I say. "Why don't you read them for me? Just for fun."

"For fun?" he asks. "The cards are a powerful oracle. Sometimes people don't like what they hear. Are you sure?"

"I'm willing to take a chance," I say, as I look at Sonny. He smiles and nods.

We pull our chairs up around a scratched thick wooden table. Don Pablo looks into my eyes, his irises as satiny black as his pupils, and in a low voice tells me to shuffle a worn, coffee-stained deck of tarot cards, then to cut them three times. He takes them from me, placing them face up on the table in rows from left to right. His wrinkled index finger sporting a filthy fingernail marks off three cards, and landing on the fourth, he calls out, "Travel, you're going to travel!" Again, he counts, "One, two, three... You're going to travel!" And then a third time the same prediction.

"I have no plans to go anywhere," I say shaking my head. "None."

"It's in the cards."

"Will Sonny be going also?"

"I read your cards, not his," he says.

Sonny stares at the cards. What was he thinking? I was leaving him? Leaving and never coming back?

"And our kids? What do the cards say about them?" I ask.

We shuffle, cut and lay out the cards in the same way as the first time, and he counts.

"One, two, three, money, they'll have lots of money."

"Will they be happy?"

"One, two, three, abundance always." And then, "The cards have nothing more to say."

At the gate Sonny gives Don Pablo some cash and he hugs us both. As we drive away, I look back and we wave, until a cloud of dust swallows him.

We're quiet as the dirt road turns onto a paved highway. Then Sonny says, "I don't know if it's true, but everyone used to say that John Cook was gay, and that Don Pablo was his lover. Maybe that's why the marriage with my mother fell through."

My thoughts are focused on Don Pablo's predictions. I'm anxious to see the world and hopeful that our kids will never need to rummage in dumpsters.

It doesn't take long for his predictions to come true.

Don Pablo's predictions about travel have come gloriously true, and our kids are thriving. I want to thank Don Pablo and tell him about our adventures as soon as possible. In April an orchestra tour to Quintana Roo, in May to Colima to play in the university orchestra and in June a concert in Tuxtla Gutierrez. Nevertheless, four years fly by before we find ourselves standing where that old rickety bamboo gate should be. Looking over the new metal gate, we're surprised to see an impeccably pruned garden and a freshly painted house. Sonny yells his name again and again, but Don Pablo never appears. Walking around the edge of the fence brings Sonny closer to the house. He yells again.

"What do you want?" asks a young man, emerging from the house.

"We've come to visit Don Pablo," Sonny says.

"He's gone. Died."

"But how? And when?" Sonny's face is white.

"He's gone, passed on to the other side," the man says. "I know nothing more."

Sonny stands at the fence staring. I take his hand; lead him back to the car.

"I know that other people were interested in that house and weren't happy that Don Pablo inherited it," Sonny says, shaking his head. "He was perfectly fine the last time we were here."

"We waited too long to thank him," I say.

2004

A SINGULAR MEETING

Life is full of surprises and serendipity. Be open to
unexpected turns in the road - Condoleeza Rice

"What did you say they hired us for?" Sonny asks, pulling
up to the iron gates at Campo Marte, the venue for
México's military and government events in Mexico City.
The place is swarming with black suits and walkie-talkies,
army trucks with mounted machine guns line the street.

"A nonprofit wants background music for a luncheon."

"Camerata de Oro Quartet," Sonny says, showing his
ID to the guard. "Why all the security?"

The guard checks a clipboard. "Park and someone will
tell you where to go."

"Stand near the tables, behind the red ribbons flanking
the aisles," a black suit says.

Soon the honorary guest arrives: Felipe Calderón, the
President of México. A blur of officials courses down the
far aisle through a flurry of waving hands and shouts of
buenos días. The president speaks for fifteen minutes,

nods to applause and then enters my aisle. His gaze entraps me. He's smiling. Sonny presses against my back.

He's closing in! What's the protocol if he stops? Do I bow? Salute? Sing the national anthem? My heart pounds in my ears. He takes my hand, pulls me close, kisses my cheek.

"How are you?" he asks.

I look back at Sonny, my eyes wide in disbelief, palms up. "See that?"

The president, sensing the awkward pause, reaches behind me to Sonny, shakes and whispers, "Congratulations."

2004

MY RIGHT ARM

Believe half of what you see and none of what you hear.
- Benjamin Franklin

I'm in the middle of five-year-old David's violin class,
when I see the doctor's number buzz on my phone. "Put
some more rosin on your bow," I say. "I need to answer
this."

"The lab found pre-cancer cells," he says. "We need to
check. Probably operate."

Not so fast! I need time to think about this. "I'd like a
second opinion," I say.

I'm worried, so I call a gynecologist, just arrived from
California.

"I don't think that's necessary," she says, the next day
at her office. She recommends a D&C (dilation and
curettage). Pointing to a color poster hanging on the wall
of a uterus, she shows me the lining she'll remove.

I'm anxious about the operation; not so much about the
surgery, as the anesthesia. Last time I almost didn't make

194

it back.

"Anesthesia has come a long way in the last thirty years," Dr. Dorothea says. "A sterilized operating room is all I need." And she schedules me for Friday.

Sonny drops me off early in the morning, the sun just lighting the sky. The maternity clinic is wedged between an orphanage and a private home. The place is sparkling and reeks of bleach. I'm the only patient, and the receptionist shows me to a closet-size room where I undress and slip into a hospital gown. I'm trembling, my palms sweaty.

Without a moment to change my mind, I cross the hall and climb onto a table in a miniature operating room. A green-gowned nurse with a face mask inserts and tapes a needle with saline drip to my right wrist. Doctor Dorothea enters the room smiling.

"You're going to be fine," she says. "It will be over in a few minutes."

I'm warm and sleepy. At my feet, the room fills with about thirty-five people. It's Sonny and the kids, my siblings, parents, friends. A liquid-warm love envelops me.

In twenty minutes, it's over, and I'm already back from the anesthesia.

The following week, I practice piano for hours and assume that's the reason for the ache in my arm. A few days later, a red line is winding up the inside of my wrist, starting from the IV entrance. Dr. Dorothea prescribes an antibiotic. Three days later, my arm is larger than a watermelon, the red line above my elbow now. There's no response to the antibiotics and my arm is about to burst. I urge Sonny to call Dr. Dorothea, and he doesn't hesitate.

He's there when I need him most.

"It's not an infection," Sonny says to her. "It's getting worse."

Finally, the doctor recommends a vein specialist. Sonny calls, and after explaining my symptoms, the doctor says it's urgent.

I have thrombosis, an intravascular coagulation of the blood. My vein was damaged by the needle.

"The clotting is out of control," the specialist says, running a finger along the red line up to my shoulder. "If it reaches the heart you'll die."

The specialist prescribes three injections, one a day. What he doesn't say, I learn later, is that they could have killed me.

I'm glad I've finally been diagnosed correctly, but I need to get the medication started as soon as possible. Sonny recognizes the urgency and drives me to a pharmacy. I ask the clerk, who sells me the Cexane, if she can inject me.

"I don't know how, but there's a lady up the street, at the shoe store," the clerk says. "She can do it for you."

I find the store, shoes and shoe boxes stacked in lopsided columns all over the floor, colorful handbags hanging from the ceiling. It smells of fresh leather and shoe polish. The woman has no cotton or alcohol, so I drag my swollen arm back to the pharmacy for essential paraphernalia. On the way back, I read the instructions on the box.

"Shouldn't you be injecting under the skin?" I ask, as she aims to jab the needle into the muscle on my upper arm. "It says, 'to be applied subcutaneously.'"

"OK. I know how to inject that way, too," she says.

196

I reread the box: "Extremely dangerous. Only to be administered in a controlled environment, such as a clinic or hospital, where the patient can be observed. Risk of bleeding to death." Minutes later, the fluid works its magic, my arm deflating like a pricked balloon.

But here I am, in a shoe store, afraid to take another step; a scrape to the knee or a grazed finger, and I can bleed to death. Why didn't the doctor warn me?

There is no option other than to brave the world with all its razor-sharp, pointed edges, so out I go.

2004

UNIQUE WEDDINGS

And above all, watch with glittering eyes the whole world around you because the greatest secrets are always hidden in the most unlikely places. Those who don't believe in magic will never find it. - Roald Dahl

The bride who wants a Disney set for her wedding gets the crown for being our most extravagant client. Even after I explain that we can arrange the repertoire and payment by phone, she insists on a meeting at her house to confirm the details.

Sonny and I pull up to a walled property in an affluent section of town and ring the bell. After a 10-minute wait, a gardener opens and ushers Sonny and me through 10-feet-tall wooden doors and up a path, huge elephant plants and ferns brushing against us. The vegetation parts, exposing an enormous brick terrace adjacent to an impressive Mexican colonial house with red-tiled roof. While we sit and wait for the hosts, a uniformed maid offers us lemonade.

I hate waiting, a demonstration of who owns whose time, whose life. After fifteen minutes, the couple arrives, and I note that the husband is at least 20 years older than his bride, Tammy. She looks about 30, shoulder-length bleached blond hair, heavy makeup, polished nails. Eyes flashing and hands fluttering, she explains her vision for the event, and with each detail, I realize this will be no ordinary celebration. Her "prince," dressed in medieval royal garb, will arrive on a white horse, accompanied by a gentleman dressed as a medieval knight, while she will arrive in an open carriage pulled by a "unicorn" (a white horse with a horn glued to his forehead). She requests songs from Disney movies: Some Day My Prince Will Come, A Dream is a Wish Your Heart Makes, Kiss the Girl and, to accompany the guests to the reception, Be Our Guest.

Tammy chatters on: "Ten men, dressed like the princess's royal guard, will form two columns ascending the wide staircase, crossing their swords to form a tunnel through which we'll pass. I've bought pageboy costumes for you musicians. You'll be on the terrace above, along with the bridesmaids, who'll be dressed like the guests at Cinderella's ball. The bridesmaids and royal guard will deliver messages of love and celebration while you'll create the perfect ambiance playing themes from Disney movies."

The groom, his gaze focused on Sonny, has been noticeably silent. Suddenly he sits upright and points. "You look exactly like Charlton Heston! I knew you looked familiar!"

"A lot of people say that," I say. "Once we were in a restaurant, and two elderly ladies at the next table kept staring at us. They finally approached our table. Sonny insisted he wasn't the famous actor, but the women said please, all they wanted was an autograph. They bubbled their gratitude when Sonny finally signed their paper placemats, wishing them much success, with much love, from "Charlton."

"And you look just like Princess Diana," the bride says, addressing me. "When I first saw you, I said, my God, it's Princess Di!"

This bride is so caught up in her princess wedding that everyone is beginning to look like royalty. We laugh and chat a good while, and then another surprise:

"I used to be a musician, too," the groom says. "I used to play gospel and rock. I was Elvis Presley's drummer." I don't believe it.

"Do you have pictures?"

"I don't know where they are, but you can see me in videos of Elvis's 1969 to 1972 World Tour." Laughing, he adds, "But I don't look as clean cut as I do now. My hair was down to my waist in those days. Our band played mostly gospel in church when we started." He goes on to say that he studied with the drummer from The Doors. I'm going to do some investigating.

After arrangements for the wedding are confirmed, the couple takes us on a tour of the grounds and shows us two rivers that flow through the property. This house originally belonged to the first Mexican scientist who specialized in plant genetics. We observe two notable specimens which he'd engineered: an albino amate tree and a cactus-palm hybrid. We're walking in the very garden where he'd conducted these experiments. Then, a metal cross at the base of a tree.

"That's where the plant genius' ashes are scattered," Tammy says.

The wedding goes off without a hitch and the guests are fascinated by the regal event.

A few years later, we're in the neighborhood and stop by the royals' house. Papers and leaves flutter around the front doors. A gardener opens. "They're gone," he says. "Left Mexico. Things didn't work out for them."

Another unique wedding takes place deep in the forest. I meet the bride and groom for the first time when they stop at our stand at a wedding expo. They're young, and both have several piercings in their eyebrows, noses and lips. Both have honey-blonde hair: hers loose to the waist, and his spiked and gelled. In relaxed hippie- style dress, they resemble Sonny and me when we were just starting

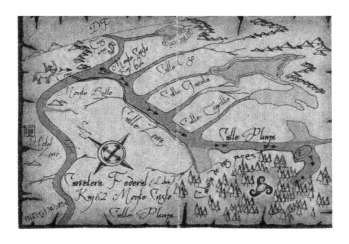

WEDDING INVITATION

out, and I take a special interest in them. They request a meeting, and I invite them over to our house for coffee, something I never do with clients.

Tamara explains that their wedding will commence at 10:00 PM. The venue is the woods, two kilometers from my house, and the guests of honor, all the forest creatures, including elves, fairies, and spirits. For the ceremony they want my quartet to play medieval music. Mauricio, the groom, hands me an invitation. We're also invited to stay and join the celebration. The invitation is homemade, with a drawing of ivy crisscrossing the envelope. Inside I read: "With profound gratitude to life, we invoke the elements to celebrate the union of our lives with the blessing of the sun, and thus give birth to a unified future of love, truth, harmony, and peace." The map is accurate, written in Merlin-era calligraphy. "Elfish, magical, fantastic medieval dress is requested," it says, and beneath, the address of a costume rental place.

The day of the wedding, I drive over to the site to be sure I'll be able to find the place later in the dark. At the end of a steep street, I park the car and then walk another 100 feet into lush foliage. Mauricio and his friends are stringing lights and setting up wooden tables and chairs, while Tamara hangs chains of flowers. "Guests will go from tree to tree to be served the banquet," Tamara says, following my gaze to the huge clay pots hanging in the trees at waist level. They look exhausted and the set-up is far from over, but it's hard not to notice the tenderness and care they feel for each other and this event.

Dressed in medieval tunics, we musicians arrive an hour early and are shown to a rickety wooden stage, uneven and dimly-lit. Towards 10:00, the full moon casts eerie forest-shadows on arriving princesses, elves, fairies, wizards, and horses: a Mexican Midsummer Night's Dream. Tamara arrives last in a simple, ankle-length, flowing white gown with a ring of flowers crowning her head, and Mauricio is at her side in prince garb. At 11:00 we're still waiting for the ceremony to begin. One of the guests stops by to say that the elves and fairies have not arrived. Finally, around midnight, the shaman unites Tamara's and Mauricio's lives in a unique ceremony while we play Scarlatti, Monteverdi and Vivaldi. Every once in a while, out of the corner of my eye, I catch a glimpse of light flashing by, or hear a scurrying in the leaves. I'm transported to another place and time, where all intentions are noble and magic reigns.

I'm so touched by their extraordinary, loving celebration that when the groom pays me, I return half of our fee as a wedding gift.

Three years and two kids later, they're divorcing. We're invited to play at the party.

Neither royalty nor forest sprites attended my wedding. There were no flowers, no music, and I'm missing an album of photos where I was queen for a day. Maybe, someday, it will happen for me.

2006

FLACA, SPIRIT ANIMAL

Let life unfold. - Anonymous

Dogs hear and smell better than humans and can even find tumors in sick patients. On an episode of 911, a man tries to walk his two German shepherds. They whine and pull towards the house until their master turns back. Just inside the back door, the man collapses of a heart attack, barely able to call the paramedics. The canines sensed that their owner's ticker was off.

The day before our planned road trip to San Antonio, Texas, Sonny takes our dogs, Sandy, Scar Face, and *Flaca*, (Skinny) up into the woods. Flaca, bounds down the path through thick brush, and out of sight. A minute later, Sonny finds her limping and by the end of the walk she's dragging her hind legs. The next morning at daybreak, Flaca is too weak to stand. I ask Danny to take her to the vet and Sonny and I leave for San Antonio.

FLACA

Just past Queretaro, around 10 A.M., we stop for gas and breakfast. It's my turn to drive and I feel safe going 75 mph on the straight-away. Just over a hill, barely time to brake, I see cars stopped in both lanes. Blood drains from my head. A red truck, tires in the air, lies in a field 20 feet off the road. Volunteers from the cars ahead are covering the faces of the scattered bodies with jackets and shirts. Sonny yells. "The goats!"

"What are you talking about? I don't see any goats!"

"That's the red truck at the gas station," he says. "The bumper sticker says, 'Go Goats,' the Guadalajara soccer team! They ate breakfast at the table next to us and I was going to tease them about how bad their team is. Now they're dead. If I had said something maybe it would have been the few minutes they needed to avoid this."

We're shaken up about the accident and arriving in San Antonio I call Danny to ask about Flaca. "The vets ran tests and gave her medicine, but they couldn't figure out what was wrong with her," Danny says. "She died on the examining table."

After we're back home, Mario, our fix-it man, comes to repair the water pump. His mother was a medicine woman in Veracruz. He can tell me the native and Spanish name for every plant on my property, and what ailment it cures. I tell him about the accident and Flaca.

"Flaca knew one of you was going to die," he says. "When did she go?"

"Around 11 in the morning, the same time as the accident."

Palms up he shrugs. "She gave her life for you. Dogs are noble like that."

I don't know what to say.

2006

A YOUTH ORCHESTRA

It's not what happens to you, but how you react to it that matters. - Epictetus

I'm jolted awake, sweating and uneasy. It's the middle of the night, early June 2006.

Fireflies enter an open window, guided by a wisp of crisp air, tiny lighthouses blinking urgency. Twenty-seven years in a cozy cabin in the forgotten town of Huitzilac, south of Mexico City, a paradise for our kids, raising rabbits and sheep, designing underground forts, picking wild berries in pine forest. Life here has been idyllic, yet something bothers me.

A whisper comes amidst crickets' raspy singing and Sonny's rhythmic snoring. It occurs to me that we have given nothing. How can we show our gratitude to this community which is, for our family, a kind of sacred place full of wondrous memories.

It's the town's saint day, Saint John the Baptist. Don Delfino invites Sonny and me to lunch at his one-room hut. We arrive a bit late to find a handful of villagers passing dishes around the long table: chicken in mole, rice, beans, and tortillas. Sonny and I are warmed by the chatter and the pulque, yet the nagging voice of my midnight epiphany returns: What more might we give?

CHRISTMAS CONCERT - ORQUESTA JUVENIL COLIBRI

As we smile our goodbyes, a skinny, wide-eyed child, legs planted wide, blocks our path. "I want to play violin," she says. She and her sisters sign up, and the orchestra is born.

ORCHESTRA PROBLEMS: INSTRUMENTS AND A VENUE

My little violinists know in their bones that what they do is unique, and the news spreads. More kids sign up. Now, we welcome new problems: the need for more instruments and a space to rehearse. Our front terrace is now the Huitzilac Cultural Center.

One day, a private student, Ceci, joins us for a group lesson. Her grandmother, Conchita, watches as five students pass two violins back and forth, taking turns playing Twinkle, Twinkle. "This sharing of violins is ridiculous!" she says. "I want to donate a violin! How much are they?"

"$1000 pesos ($100 dollars)," I say.

"I'll donate two," she says.

One Sunday, I schedule our little ensemble to play at St. Michael's Church: Pachelbel Canon for the prelude, Dona Nobis for communion and Ode to Joy while the congregation shuffles out. The minister announces that today's offering will be donated to the orchestra. It's enough for another violin!

I'm thinking bread and fish now. Miracles: the Girl Scouts donate a violin a visitor left behind; Joaquin donates two violins and a cello honoring his daughter, Crystal, who, under my guidance, took to the violin like a hummingbird to bougainvillea; Victor and Andres outgrow their half-size violins and pass them on to the next generation of eager fingers.

Patrons are everywhere. On a midnight flight from London to New York, I strike up a conversation with a grey-haired lady across the aisle. I rave about the orchestra. As the plane touches down, she presses five $20 bills into my hand. "Use this for your orchestra," she says. "I wish I had more."

RISKING JAIL TIME

This orchestra mission has such a hold on me that I'm

willing to break the law, like a common criminal, and risk jail time.

At Customs at the Mexico City Airport, everyone pushes a button. If it's green, one is free to go. That day, the dreaded red light flashes. I didn't declare the instruments; I know they can seize my loot. The stern-looking official, her laced-up black boots squeaking on the marble, walks slowly over to the stainless-steel table, eyes on my bulging bags. Her black hair is slicked back in a ponytail, her uniform so tight it looks painted on, about my age, but masculine and tough. I glance around: the customs area is empty, and along the far wall, about thirty feet away, eight officials chat. I sweat. If she calls them, it's over! Should I bribe her?

Madame Pitbull points to my luggage. Shaking, I unzip the old tattered suitcase, feeble dreams like dying embers.

"What are those?" she asks, glaring at the two ¼-size violins.

"They're toys," I squeak a whisper. (I know that five used toys are allowed without import tax, but only one musical instrument.) Is she reading my mind?

"And what's that in your hand?"

"It's a viola," I answer, heat rising from my chest, my mouth dry.

"Open it!" she orders, shaking her head. "And what's in that box?"

"It's a piano keyboard, here's a picture on the box," I answer weakly, knowing that this could get jailhouse serious.

"Open it!"

I slide the keyboard slowly into view as if delivering a baby.

"What's with all these instruments?" she says.

I'm trembling. "My husband and I give music lessons to kids in a village near where we live. They don't have money. Stores in Mexico don't sell miniature violins. Playing a musical instrument improves kids' self-esteem, they learn discipline and cooperation. Music is the language of the spirit; it helps them connect with their souls." On and on I yak trying to convince this woman that it's not a crime to give back.

"Adelante, Maestra. ¡Qué le vaya bien!" Go ahead, maestra. Hope things go well for you, she smiles. I breathe.

REHEARSAL ORQUESTA JUVENIL COLIBRI

POPCORN CONCERT

Tomorrow the orchestra will perform a summer concert on our front terrace, but there's a problem. For the last ten days I've been begging Sonny to remove his tools, the horse's saddle and 50-pound bags of feed from the "concert hall," but it still looks like a hardware store.

"Will you please clean the terrace today?" I ask. "I'm going to Sally's party."

"I told you I'll take care of it!" he says.

I stash violins and violas in the dressing room of my mind; no need to think about the concert until curtain time tomorrow.

For a few wine-drenched hours I laugh and gossip with old friends, but as dusk settles, I feel uneasy. What if Sonny didn't clean up? I rush home and find the terrace as I left it hours earlier. I sigh and shake my head; a tear burns my cheek.

For the next four hours I clean, a simmering pressure cooker with no release valve. With a sweep of my arm across the tables, screw drivers, horse reins and greasy rags fall into giant dog food bags. I carry giant clamps, machetes and a weed whacker to the edge of the woods and, with the wrath of a scorned woman, I hurl them into knee-high brush, with all my strength. Fury bubbles in me as I sweep away sawdust and dog hairs and polish the wooden chairs down to raw wood.

Just as the sun is setting, Sonny gallops in on his horse. "Where's all my stuff?"

"Out there," I say, pointing to the woods.

"You've got to be out of your mind."

I call twenty-six-year-old Roxy, and ask if she can watch our grandkids, Maya (6) and Angelo (4), during the concert. "I hope that, after hearing our little orchestra perform, they'll scramble to practice their violins," I say. "Make sure they stay for the whole thing."

"You know you can always count on me, Mom."

The day of the concert, a handful of parents arrive early, like angels bearing extra chairs. The miniature musicians look exquisite, jet-black gel-styled hair, freshly pressed dresses and suites.

The kids line up and I tune fifteen violins, four violas, three cellos, and a double bass. We're five minutes from show time and Sonny has something to tell me.

"My new cello student, Irma, will be playing with us."

"She's a beginner. She hasn't rehearsed!"

"She'll do fine," he says.

Sonny and Irma set up near the cellos. They join in on the first number, but by the second line, Irma is lost. She stops and shakes her head at the audience, breaking the first rule of all musicians: When in doubt, fake it. Irma distracts Sonny. He's lost now. Remember the rule! He stumbles on, wrong note after wrong note, throwing the violins into a blundering cacophony. The audience claps and the kids take a bow. The next selection, Sonny and his student try again. This time they're playing in a different key!

With no one to watch them, Maya and Angelo sneak back into our bedroom and switch on The Sound of Music. Half an hour into the concert, Roxy finally arrives. We're no match for María and the Von Trapp Family.

My piano is in the foyer of my house, the stage now for the solo numbers, the kitchen right behind. I'm on piano, accompanying seven-year-old Vanesa's solo violin, when suddenly the sound of metal sliding over metal. There is no percussion in this piece! Behind us, 25-year-old Danny slides a pot back and forth on the stove. Then, adding color to Danny's rhythm section, the corn begins popping. I shake my head. The piece finished, I rush to the stove.

"Do you have any idea what we're doing here? This is a formal concert!"

"Hold on Mom. Popcorn's almost done. Don't get all freaked." Then: "Anyone want some?" as he weaves his way through the audience to an empty chair.

After the concert, parents celebrate their kids with mini bouquets of red roses, homemade mango juice, tuna sandwiches, and a chocolate cake. *Felicidades Orquesta!,* Congratulations Orchestra! it says, with dancing notes and melting violin decorations. Pictures of beaming kids with their parents embracing them will capture the essence of this moment. No one will remember the wrong notes or the popcorn incident.

ANGEL AND THE ACCIDENT

I've just finished tuning the violins for our afternoon rehearsal, when Susana, a cello student, runs up the driveway. She's out of breath. "It's Angel! A car hit him and he's lying by the side of the road. My parents are with him."

Blood drains from my head. Angel, 14, just started violin classes this month.

"Is he breathing?" I ask.

"His leg is sticking out through his skin!"

"Is he alive?" I ask, ready to shake her.

Sonny is rehearsing the cellos and I run behind the house to tell him. "Go see what's happened," I say. "Alone. No need for a bunch of hysterical kids down there."

Sonny dashes off and Susana fills us in: A friend gave Angel and his cousin a ride down from the village. He let them out on the highway. A teenager, screeching around the curve, lost control and hit Angel, already halfway across."

Sonny is back for his motorcycle. The ambulance will take Angel to the hospital and Sonny will follow behind.

I run scales on the piano, walk out to the gate, drink tea, play more scales, waiting for news. Almost midnight, Sonny calls. The driver was insured so Angel is in surgery at Inovamed, an upscale private hospital. He has a private room with a bathroom and TV. Hope this eases some of the pain. Home is a dirt-floor shack.

"This is a warning," Sonny says. "The kids risk their lives every time they come to class."

"The highway is dangerous, but so is the world," I say. "I'm not giving up."

ANGEL AND PANCHO

This is the second summer that the government awards me a generous grant for my summer orchestra day-camp. Forty kids at my house every day for five weeks. What could go wrong?

"We're hiking to the soccer field for today's activity," I tell the kids one afternoon. Sonny decides Pancho, his horse, is going.

"We've come here to play kickball," I say when we arrive. "Let's set up. No one on the horse!" The kids throw down jackets to mark the bases and home plate. We're choosing teams (beginning orchestra against advanced), when Ana yells, "Look! Ángel!"

Sonny is holding the reins and Angel, the boy who six months ago was hit by a car, beams from atop Pancho. Timid Angel, who struggles with the violin, but never misses class, who speaks to no one, but laughs at all the jokes. Angel enjoys the camaraderie and now he's the center of attention.

"What are you doing?" I ask Sonny, trying to mask my frustration. "Why don't you play kickball with us? No one should ride Pancho. He comes here to run."

"They're having fun," Sonny says.

I won't argue in front of the kids and turn my back on the rebellious trio. "Beginners up to kick first," I say. And then, Pancho galloping. Angel flies by, eyes shut, reins flapping.

"Grab the reins, grab the reins!" Sonny yells.

"He can't! They're loose!" I scream.

Angel strangles the pommel; his long legs crush the horse's ribs. The kids freeze, mouths agape. Silence, save for the sound of pounding hooves and heavy brute breathing. Pancho is not stopping. On the second lap Angel is white, his eyes still pinched, face grotesquely twisted.

"Do something, Sonny! Do something!" I cry.

Sonny reaches out and grabs the reins as the horse gallops by. Leather whips from his hand, bones snap. On the third lap, Brandon, a bass student, waves his arms. "Whoa, whoa," he says in a deep tenor. Pancho slows, then stops. Smiling, Angel alights to hugs and applause. A hero. I'm shaking, my legs collapse, and I drop to my knees.

"Let's go back," I call out after a minute. "This is just too much responsibility."

I don't speak to Sonny for three days.

"Nothing happened," he says. "And for Angel, it was an experience he'll never forget."

It's true. The other kids are in awe of this boy, so shy

that he'd turn red as a traffic light if anyone even looked at him. He rode the wind and survived. His self-esteem is soaring. And Sonny broke bones to save this child. I forgive him.

NO PARENTS ALLOWED!

With only twenty students, Sonny and I do it all: put up stands and chairs, break up bow-fighting, and supply forgotten music. But two years later, the orchestra has grown to fifty, we need help. Who better than the parents?

At one village concert, I ask parents to help set up, but as soon as the bus stops, everyone dashes for the door and disappears like bandits fleeing a bungled bank heist. With no time to argue, Sonny and I hustle to convert the outdoor cement basket-ball court into an orchestra stage.

After the last applause dies out, the municipal president invites us to a homemade dinner. In a frenzy, parents grab their kids and rush off to the town hall, leaving half-opened cases and scattered music in their wake. Sonny and I take down the stage and arrive last at the mess hall. All the parents are seated, their snouts twitching, a handful of students standing.

"Can you please let the kids eat?" I ask at the first table.

The organizers scurry around, setting up more tables and chairs. "Don't worry," one of them whispers, rushing by. "We're used to town folk. We made lots of food."

Not enough it seems. Some little ones are handed a tortilla with a dab of macaroni.

"Those ladies told us to sit," the head sow squeals. They refuse to yield to the little ones.

On the bus ride back, the adrenalin-crazed kids run up and down the aisles of the bus, others dangle heads and hands out the windows, laughing and shouting. Parents chat, oblivious. From now on, no parents allowed.

A GIFT FOR THE ORCHESTRA

The last day of May, the phone rings just as I'm opening my eyes. It can only be bad news at this hour.

"Where do you live? It says Huitzilac Road, but would that be on the north or south side of the village?"

"Who is this?" I ask.

The agitated voice says they have a delivery for me. But I'm not expecting anything.

"We have a delivery of musical instruments. We can't find your street."

"Come down through the town and I'll run down to the highway and wait for you."

Ten minutes later, a truck turns into our dusty road. I'm breathless, hoping that after years of stalking the government they've finally coughed up a few violins, maybe a flute or a couple of trumpets. The truck gets caught up in a low-hanging tangle of illegal electrical wires, blocking access for delivery.

"How many instruments?" I ask, as the driver walks around to the back of the truck.

He smiles and flings open the doors, the inside solid boxes of all shapes and sizes. "They're all yours!" he says. "All 84!"

Sonny jumps right in and makes eight trips with his blue pick-up truck down to the road for the instruments. We fill our living space with an orchestra: thirty-four violins, twelve violas, twelve cellos, five basses, a keyboard, three flutes, three oboes, four clarinets, two bassoons, five French horns, three trumpets, two trombones, thirty music stands, a podium: an orchestra director's gold mine.

"Who sent this?" I ask.

"The president had a little extra cash, and he needed to spend it before the end of May. I guess he likes music," he laughs.

My house is a disaster, instruments everywhere, a welcome mess.

WHY PRACTICE?

More kids sign up, performances all over the state, week-long orchestra camps in Queretaro, Guadalajara and Guanajuato, and then, it's over. A new government has come to power. The person appointed to coordinate the national orchestra system needs to repay favors to a famous Mexican composer. The composer's wife, Lorena, has no musical training but wants an orchestra. She doesn't know a quarter note from a squashed fly.

In September 2013 Lorena calls.

"I've just been appointed the Academic Coordinator of Orchestras in the state," she says. "I want a detailed report of every one of your classes. Every week."

"That's 13 classes a week," I say. "Do you want me to teach or write reports?"

A week later, Lorena bursts into my orchestra rehearsal unannounced. She's dressed in platform shoes, a tight shirt and mini skirt, long dangling earrings. After observing me for a few minutes she interrupts: "Come outside. I need to talk to you!" In the hall she continues. "You're not teaching social skills through the music," she says. "When you talked about crescendo and diminuendo, you didn't explain to the students how every day they have crescendos and diminuendos. How will they deal with them?"

"We talk about how important it is to finish school, to have a career and not have babies at 14 or 15, especially the girls," I say. "Here's the baton," I say. "Show me what you want."

"Now you're challenging me?" Lorena says. "Unacceptable. It's obvious you don't know how to teach, much less play the violin."

Lorena sends a report to the National Coordinator and then demands a meeting:

"Since you're unwilling to use our methodology, we're withdrawing support for the orchestra at the end of the year. You can keep the instruments. For now."

"Instruments, but no teachers?"

By the end of the year the five orchestras in the state withdraw from the National System. The government gives Lorena instruments and salaries for teachers so she can start her own orchestra at a boarding school in town. But she can't find qualified teachers to work for her.

"Why should I practice?" Luis, a 12-year-old cellist in our orchestra says, when he hears of Lorena's windfall. "You don't need to know anything to have an orchestra. You just have to know the right people."

"But how will you feel about *yourself* if you do that?" I say.

I don't wait long for Lorena to realize she was wrong about me. Her partner, the composer, directs a youth orchestra for some of the best players in the state. At the first concert, they approach the concertmistress, Valeria. "Congratulations," Lorena says, shaking her hand. "You played beautifully. Who is your teacher?"

"I'm from Huitzilac," Valeria says. "It's Laurie."

Lorena nods and they move on to the principal players of the other sections.

The answer is always the same.

ONE LAST FLING

The new national orchestra coordinator honors the travel arrangements I made with the previous government and pays for plane tickets for our tour to Cancun and Tulum. And there are others who help make our dream a reality: The town of Huitzilac provides transportation to and from the airport, the state pays for local transportation around Cancun, the city of Tulum pays for our meals and we stay at a hotel ten feet from the waves of the Atlantic, courtesy of Diamante K Hotel.

Fifteen kids and four adults bubble with excitement as we head for the Cuernavaca Airport. At the ticket counter the woman with painted-on eyebrows and thick red lipstick orders me to de-string the instruments, with the argument that my eight-year-olds will use them to strangle the pilots. I refuse.

"Do as you like, but I know security won't let you on with those things," the lady says.

I'm first in line at the conveyor belt and launch my defense. "Isn't it amazing? These kids are from Huitzilac. That village up in the hills? We're on tour. Going to Tulum and Cancun. These are talented kids. You should hear them play. We've got a great program, La Negra, The Pink Panther, Can-Can."

"Instruments on the belt," the officer says, a big smile to the kids.

There's no mention of strangling strings. A nightmare of restringing fourteen instruments has been avoided.

My sparkling daughter Roxy is there to greet us. She's arranged the meals, local transportation and a hotel in Tulum. The kids want to see the ocean. Five minutes later they're splashing in the waves. In their concert clothes!

The rehearsal and performance in Cancun with a local youth choir go off without a hitch, the conductor Noe beaming as he treats us to enchiladas at a local restaurant. Then we're off on the two-hour ride to Tulum.

The kids are speechless when they spill from the van into the hotel.

"The huts are made of bamboo!" they whisper. "The beds swing from ropes!" "The bathrooms have no doors! We can't stay here!"

"Yeah," Roxy says. "People shell out $300 dollars a night for these shacks."

ORQUESTA JUVENIL COLIBRI IN TULUM, MEXICO

By the following morning, the kids are in love with their new home: the smell and sounds of the saltwater, the cool breeze whispering through the palm trees, the hammocks swaying. A tour of the pyramids followed by our concert at the hotel, fill the day.

Our last performance is at the Tulum Cultural Center. After the final applause dies down, I announce that all the instruments we have performed on will be donated to the town of Tulum.

"These instruments were donationed to the orchestra by people who believed they would change lives. And they have. Now, we pass them on to this community." We'd chosen Tulum, which had been so good to our daughter. Each member of the orchestra hands their instrument to a child in the audience who climbs on stage to receive it.

Huitzilac does not fail us on our return trip. A van is awaiting us at the Mexico City Airport to transport us home. We hang the banner announcing our Tulum concert out the window at the cultural center. Two days later it disappears.

In December 2015, Sonny and I announce we're leaving the orchestra. Ten years of an enriching experience has ended.

As the last note of our final concert evaporates into silence, like the gentle turning of the last page of a profoundly stirring symphony score, I take the microphone: "Thank you, to my faithful husband for supporting me in this project. Thanks to you, parents, for lending me your kids, beautiful souls who enriched my life."

And to the orchestra: "Think of angels. What do you

see? Harps, trumpets, violins. You are angels. Godspeed."

THE FIGHT FOR MUSIC CONTINUES

A few weeks into the semester the new director calls.
The youth orchestra is floundering. Will Sonny and I
consider going once a week to help with the string
sections. Of course we will.

Halfway through a rehearsal, a young man, dressed in
suit and tie knocks on the door. He asks to see me in the
hall. "It will only take a minute."

He hands me an official looking document from the
federal prosecutor's office. "You're being accused of
theft," he says. "According to Efrain, director of youth
orchestras in Mexico, you stole 84 instruments from the
federal government. Report to the authorities the day after
tomorrow to state your defense."

Am I hallucinating? "Look in the room," I say. "The
instruments are there."

"I'm just delivering the summons," he says.

"I'm going with you," Sonny says. "This is ridiculous.
We've invited Efrain to every concert and he never came
even once."

A twelve-foot-high concrete wall surrounds the federal
building, metal doors at the entrance with a square-foot
door at face level. We knock and show ID. Once inside
an armed guard searches our bags and runs a metal
detector around our bodies. "No computers and no minors
allowed," he says.

Inside we pass through airport-style security and then
show IDs again at a lobby desk. Fifteen or so machine-
gun-armed guards mill about. A few minutes later, a
young woman, light hair in a bun, dressed in a suit and

high-heels, greets us and shows us to her office.

In fifteen minutes, Sonny and I explain our youth orchestra project. "There are narcos, arms dealers, illegal loggers, and I'm here for an orchestra project?" I say.

The woman rolls her eyes and shakes her head. This feels so surreal. I'm lightheaded.

"You can come hear a concert, see the instruments, anytime," I say. "This weekend we have a joint concert with Tepoztlán."

TEPOZTLAN AND HUITZILAC YOUTH
ORCHESTRA CONCERT

A month later, federal police are waiting at the cultural center with another stamped and sealed document. It's a reduced list. Now, they say, I've only stolen five instruments: an accordion, two bugles, a guitar and a bongo. I open the filing cabinet and draw a folder with the list of instruments I received from the Secretary of

Culture.

"These are not on the list," I say. "We don't use them in an orchestra."

Each policeman holds a sheet and they compare, heads jerking side to side. I gaze at the guns hanging from their hips and the machine guns slung on their backs. A lot of firepower just to take away our music.

The men mutter. "They're not on the list." "This is ridiculous." "A waste of time."

"We're sorry to bother you," one says. The other rolls his eyes. They shake their heads and turn. "Pardon us," he says. "We'll be going now and won't bother you again."

2006

CONCERTS FOR KIDS

Difficult things take a long time, impossible things a little longer. - A. Jackson

Oaxaca City, eight hours away, is the first stop on our seventeen-day concert tour. Judith, our pianist, Roxy, Danny and I lead the way in a black Pointer. Sonny and Beto, our principal actor, lag behind in a blue Nissan truck packed with a collapsible shadow theater, a life-size plastic skeleton, brooms with buckets, a treasure chest, double bass, electric piano and a violin.

The drive is easy compared to finding the theater. Cars parked sideways block the streets, and white sheets hanging across the roads proclaim a teachers' strike in dripping-red letters. I call the contact person from a payphone in a store parking lot.

"I have bad news and good news," he says. "Bad news is you won't be able to perform at the theater in town, good news: we found a basketball court that's available in a low-income apartment complex."

An open-air ball court was not what I had in mind when the Morelos Cultural Institute hired us to perform my traveling musical theater show, *el Aprendiz,* The Apprentice. But we're on a mission to introduce children to classical music, and we'll perform in a parking lot if we have to.

As we set up the shadow-theater screen, I notice dark clouds moving in. "We need to hurry," I tell Beto, zipping his blue robe spattered with silver stars. Danny, the apprentice, pulls a full-length purple tunic over his head and Roxy, dressed in a long black dress for her dance numbers, hangs the brooms on the back of the curtains. Judith warms up with scales and Sonny checks our stand lights. Behind the seven-by-ten-foot screen Sonny and I made from PVC pipes, old black curtains and a white sheet, I tack up the order of the pieces we'll perform and the magic object the apprentice will take. "This will remind you what story we're on," I say.

The Sorcerer's Apprentice
In the Hall of the Mountain King - Magic Disappearing Cape
Phantom of the Opera - Magic Mirror
Amor Brujo - Magic Lantern
Melody from Orpheus – Magic Flute
Valse Triste - Magic Potion
Funeral March - Magic Flowers
Danse Macabre - Magic Violin
Water Music - Book of Spells and Pointed Cap

"After I explain each task, exit left, around to the back

of the screen," Beto tells Danny. "And have the hatchet ready."

FUNDACIÓN DE PARQUES Y MUSEOS DE COZUMEL
presenta

CONCIERTO-TEATRO DIDÁCTICO
POR CAMERATA DE ORO Y TEATRO MUSICAL EN-CANTADO

Las Siete Pruebas del Aprendiz

Los 3 músicos y el mago tienen todo planeado para que el aprendiz pase las siete pruebas que tiene que superar para convertirse en mago...

Viernes 5 de Noviembre, 20:00 hrs
Sábado 6 de Noviembre, 19:00 hrs
¡Para toda la Familia!
Auditorio "Lic Pedro Joaquín Coldwell"
MUSEO DE LA ISLA

Interpretando música de L. Van Beethoven, A. Weber, G. Handel, J. Sibelius entre otras

THE APPRENTICE AND THE SEVEN TASKS

Meanwhile, a handful of men with metal folding chairs appear and set up twenty crooked rows facing the stage. As the sun sets, people of all ages wander into the makeshift auditorium and take seats, eyeing the wizard's "workshop," a table crammed with skulls and candles, leather-bound books and green potions.

It's time to begin! From backstage, three of us scurry into the workshop and take seats, stage left. Before the wizard changed us into musicians, we enjoyed uneventful lives as a lizard, a parrot and a black cat. Now, the wizard insists we provide musical accompaniment for the seven tasks the apprentice must complete to receive his cap and book of spells. The wizard will explain all this in good time.

JUDITH, DANIEL, ALBERTO, LAURIE, ROXY, SONNY - THE APPRENTICE AND THE SEVEN TASKS

No sooner does the apprentice embark on his first task, then the wind picks up. As I play my violin, I notice Beto, peeking from behind the curtains. "It's impossible," he mouths. "The set is blowing away and the lights are about to collapse!"

The billowing structure is now a careening sailboat, sliding across the cement court towards the audience. I stop the music and jump to my feet. "Please, are there any volunteers who could hold our theater down, so it doesn't blow away?"

Twenty hands go up. Two men hold the free-spirited theater in place, clothespins secure our music, and the wind howls and whips through the production. It's a struggle, but we finish, and bubbling children come running to grab the wizard's robe and beg for magic classes.

The next day we drive right up to the Regional Children's Museum of Santa Ana del Valle for our next engagement, and easily find the contact person, Primo. He leads us to a cinder block house with a cactus garden front yard. We climb to the second floor where he invites us to take a place at a long blue table, red geraniums in tin cans down the center. His wife and daughters serve us green salsa tamales and warm mint tea. I notice a full-page article from the Travel Section of the New York Times on the wall in a glass frame. I look at our host, Primo, and back at the picture. "That's you!" I say.

He nods. "For six generations my family has been weaving blankets and rugs with designs like the engravings on the local pyramids," he says. "Even students from the United States come to learn about traditional weaving and dyeing."

"It's an honor to be your guests," I say. I buy two bath-size rugs. $80 US dollars each.

There's no wind and that night the performance is flawless. The children, a few at a time, approach the stage as the performance advances, some sitting others hanging on the edge of the stage.

The following day, we drive through miles of desert towards our next stop, San Juan Ixcaquixtla, Puebla. On the way, like a mirage, The Water Museum springs from the sand. We stop and explore this oasis of environmental consciousness.

After another successful concert in San Juan Ixcaquixtla, the municipal president, Don Rodolfo, and his entourage invite us for tequila and tacos. They chatter about "the discovery."

"In April 2004, a truck with cement drove into a client's yard, and sunk to its belly," Rodolfo says, pouring a drink. "The truck had fallen into an ancient burial site with bones and artifacts. Intact." He throws his head back and swallows from the shot glass. "Digging farther, three tombs were uncovered, with four skeletons and fifty-one clay pitchers and bowls. The priests' tombs most likely."

"When villages in this area got word that the Spanish conquistadores were on the horizon, they'd bury the sacred sites, cover them with dirt and brush, make them look like ordinary hills," his friend says. "Let's go see it."

In less than a half hour we arrive at the site, but a chain and padlock on metal doors block the entrance. We peek through a crack in the doors but see nothing.

An icy breeze brushes my arms. I shiver. If we interfaced with a time warp, what would we see? A civilization desperately fighting to stave off the inevitable ravaging of an entire population. "We'll see it on our next trip," I say.

Judith can't perform the next concert in Cuauhtinchán, Puebla. "I have another commitment," she says. I can't waste time or energy getting upset about Judith's lack of

232

professionalism. We can't do The Apprentice without piano, but we can do another show I wrote. Albert, Live!, a contemporary musical in talk-show format. I´ll add the violin melody as I play the recorded accompaniment on the piano and, with Sonny on bass, we're covered. I call Gaby, the "opera star" in the show.

DANIEL, ALBERTO, GABY, JUDITH, LAURIE,
SONNY - ALBERT, LIVE!

The stage is a flimsy, wooden-planked, three-foot-high structure in the center of the main plaza, with only a tarp to protect us from the elements. Beto, the host of the talk show, uses a microphone to introduce his two guests, an opera singer (Gaby) and a rock-and-roll, break-dancer, rapper (Danny on guitar), who argue about which is the best song of all time by playing, singing and dancing a tango, a waltz, an aria, a movie theme, a ballet, rock and roll, and an original piece by Danny. But the wind whips away most of the dialogue. Only the music survives. The audience applauds anyway and a few approach the stage, some shake hands, others just stare and shake their heads. "Only two people made that great music?" one asks.

This town boasts a sixteenth-century convent, modeled after a medieval castle. We take a tour and climb to the top of the bell tower to look down on fields of corn and the town square.

For our engagement the next day, there is no one to meet us at the open -air theater at the town square in Tlaxcala, and our contact person doesn't answer his phone.

"We have a performance here in town," I say to the traffic policeman at the town square.

"You can't stop and unload here," he says, waving his arms to direct traffic around our car-truck caravan. "No one told me of any presentation."

The wind picks up, papers and garbage cans roll down the street. We need an enclosed venue. An hour later, the policeman almost convinced, our contact person arrives.

"The committee wants you to perform outside. That's where the townspeople congregate. It's hard to get villagers inside for any kind of performance

"Does this town even have a real theater?" I ask. "It's going to rain."

"It's just a few blocks from here," he says, pointing down the street.

We enter the Xicotencatl Theater through doors behind the stage and, as I walk out to the edge and peer out at the empty seats, I'm speechless. It's a mini Bellas Artes,

Marie Antoinette's Theater at Versailles, the Philadelphia Music Academy. It's more beautiful still: a hardwood professional stage, red velvet curtains and seats, gold-painted banisters and decoration. "It's magnificent," I sigh.

"Yes," contact man says. "But how are we going to get the people in here?"

"Leave it to us," I say.

Right after we set up, Beto and Danny, in full costume, march through the square. "Come one, come all," Beto says. "Will the boy complete the tasks? Will he become a wizard? Come see for yourself!" Twenty minutes later, they arrive at the theater, a long line of curious concert goers behind. The hushed group packs the theater, children giggle and cheer the apprentice through difficult challenges, jumping from their seats in bursts of clapping when he succeeds.

We call ahead to every town and ask the organizers to reserve rooms for us in decent hotels, which we pay on arrival. In Tlaxcala, no one honors our request, and all hotels in town are swarming with basketball players in town for a playoff. At midnight, not a room to be found, we start out for the next host city. Two miles later I spot an "auto hotel," which rents by the hour. I convince the owner to give us two rooms. "But only until sunrise," he says.

The pyramids of Cacaxtla are nearby so we spend the next morning at one of the best-preserved pre-Hispanic sites in Mexico. The original vivid red and blue painted murals adorning the buildings are protected by 10,000-square-meters of metal roof. It's breathtaking.

According to the villagers, the Morelos Cultural Institute told them of our arrival only a day before.

There's no publicity, yet with Beto and Danny's Pied Piper routine, audiences are assembled in a matter of minutes.

In San Agustin Tlajiaca, neither Judith nor Roxy can perform. Time for another of my productions: *Ensayo General!* Dress Rehearsal! A rock guitarist, a versatile violinist and a double bassist from a salsa band "rehearse" with their egocentric director. Dressed in tails and white gloves, he taps his baton to keep order, while the unruly musicians joke and chat about the composers and pieces on the program. Even the guitarist's phone interrupts, with a Bach Partita ringtone.

We're warned to be careful of thieves and con men in the impoverished towns of Ciudad Nezahualcóyotl and Texcoco, in the State of Mexico. But we encounter no thugs. In fact, we play in high-school size auditoriums packed with well-behaved, delighted school children.

Our last performance is in Mexico City, the largest city in the world. No problems with performing here, I think. We're back to civilization. But I'm wrong.

All the parking places at the stage entrance to the Benito Juarez Theater are taken, even though the place is deserted. Sonny must park on the street, but the meters only allow for 45 minutes and the concert runs an hour. By the time we bow to the applause and Sonny rushes out of the theater, there's a boot on the front tire.

"You didn't say you needed a place to unload or to park when you sent us the requirements," the organizer says.

"I didn't say we needed someone to turn on lights, open the doors to the public or take tickets either," I say. "I thought that was standard practice." Live and learn.

We wait several hours for the traffic police to turn in his report and pay the $50 dollar fine. An officer shows up an hour later to remove the chunk of metal on the tire. I'm exhausted.

Finally, the tour is over. We deliver the hand-written rave reviews from the villages to the Cultural Institute. And now, payment problems. Pre-tour, the Institute gave us $1,000 dollars cash for gas, food, and hotels. They owe us another $1,000 dollars.

"We discounted $250 dollars for your car insurance," Marilu, the treasurer, says, handing me $750 in cash.

I ask to see the policy. "The insurance took effect three days ago," I say. "We've been on the road for seventeen."

She shakes her head.

When I ask her if she wants a receipt, she says no. "How will you prove how you spent the grant money for the *Alas y Raices*, Wings and Roots project?"

"We don't have to," she says.

Yes, I'd learned that's the way it is in Mexico - bad organization, casually broken commitments, and shady financial dealings. But our mission was to take music to the masses, especially to the children, and we did.

2007

MAYA'S ROYAL BIRTHDAY

You are made of stardust and wishes and magical things.
- Anonymous

I send invitations to my granddaughter, Maya's friends and family. She is the sweet daughter of our son Pete. They are invited to celebrate Maya's 6th birthday at the castle, where Sleeping Beauty suffered that most unfortunate accident with the spinning wheel.

In the village of Huitzilac, rising above the one-room cinder block huts, stands a Medieval stone castle with storybook towers. On a grassy area the size of a football field, surrounded by a ten-foot wall, visitors gain access through two huge wooden doors and a 100-foot winding cobblestone road.

The 70-year-old owner, his niece, and her husband are my friends and agree to lend me the castle on one condition: the owner will attend as Merlin, the couple as the princess Aurora and her prince. I dream: Merlin, decked out in wizard garb, will be on hand to receive the guests. From the main hall I'll call the kid's attention to the gothic window facing the main gate, where they'll witness the prince approaching on his stallion (our horse, Pancho) at a breakneck gallop. Then, after he proves his "prince hood," as Arthur once did, pulling the sword from the stone, I'll lead Maya and her guests up the stone stairway to the upper-tower, where the prince will awaken his spell-bound beloved with a kiss.

Maya and her guests (15 kids between the ages of 5 and 10), are not only punctual but stunning: fancy pastel dresses of chiffon and satin, sparkling crowns, the boys with slicked back hair and shining shoes. They tip-toe into the main hall, gazing wide-eyed at two giant glass chandeliers, 16th century paintings of saints and angels, metal spears and hatchets on the walls, shying away from the suits of armor standing guard on either side of the front door.

An hour later there's still no sign of Aurora or Merlin. The kids shouldn't see Aurora arriving in a Volkswagen Bug! I lead the kids and their parents downstairs to the dungeon, a room the size of a classroom with a five-foot fireplace and overstuffed furniture. The parents serve the "banquet" (sandwiches, fruit and Jell-O) in the dungeon, while Sonny waits with Pancho grazing outside the front gate. What's keeping the royal couple and Merlin? I said two o'clock, it's already after three! Time is fluid here. I need to breathe.

Merlin finally arrives - a half-bottle of wine in one hand and a full glass in the other.

"I can't find my hat," he mutters, stumbling from the backseat of the car, his driver rushing to grab his elbow. The old guy's really taken his role as wizard seriously, I think, eying his long cobalt-blue robe spattered with silver stars, long white hair and beard to his waist. "Where are the kids?" he says. The driver guides Merlin through the arched ten-foot wooden doors, across the stone-floor foyer, and into the main hall, dropping him into one of several sofas.

"The only thing you have to say is 'There's a princess in this castle!'" I say.

Merlin nods his head. "Bring me the kids!" he says.

I fetch two six-year-olds from the dungeon. "We love you!" one says, hugging Merlin.

Merlin beams and asks if they'd like to see some magic.

Please no! "I hear that there's a princess asleep in this castle," I say. "That true?"

"Yes, hic, yes...of course she is," he says, leaning so far forward the kids on either side try to prop him up. "Take me to her!" he burps.

Finally, "the princess" arrives. I whisk Aurora up the tower's back stairs and open the bedroom door. "Lie down," I say. "And don't breathe!"

Then, I invite the kids into the main hall. Out the window I signal the waiting prince to charge the castle. "Look!" I say. "A prince! On a horse!" The kids clatter first to the window and then rush outside to greet him.

The prince, gold chains around his neck, boots up to his knees, long hair flowing, shouts from his horse: "Where is my princess?"

Maya's young guests, wide-eyed, faces flushed, form a circle around the horse.

"First things first," I say. "You have to prove you're a prince."

"Of course I am, just look at me," he says, circling on his stallion.

"Come this way." I say, and lead him to the sword, stuck deep into a pile of rocks, the kids running behind. "Pull this out."

The kids clap and cheer, "PRINCIPE! PRINCIPE! PRINCIPE!"

The prince yanks and tugs, grunts and groans. I shake my head. Why can't he pull the damn thing out? Pull harder! I didn't put it in that deep! Finally, it's free and he swings the shining 16th century relic above his head, as if charging into battle. The kids applaud and dance around.

"Where is my princess?" he yells. "Lead me to her!"

Into the castle and up a wide, spiraling stone stairway I lead them to a closed door, a skeleton key in the lock. I knock. The kids tremble, hugging each other, whispering. I turn the key and the door creaks open. There she lies in the four-poster bed, deep asleep, arms crossed over her chest, in a full-length purple satin dress, long hair spread out on the pillow. "She forgot to take her shoes off!" one of the kids whispers.

"I know what she needs," says the prince. He pounces on the bed, straddling the sleeping beauty and kisses her on the lips. It's more than a generic, break-a-spell kiss. "That's good," I say. Then, "The kiss worked, she's awake!" And finally, "STOP THE KISSING!"

The princess's eyelashes flicker. Maya jumps up and down, clapping her hands. The princess, after yawning and stretching, turns and says, "I have the feeling that someone in this very room is having a birthday. Who could it be?"

"It's me!" Maya says, hugging the princess. "I love

you!"

"I love you too," the princess laughs.   She takes a miniature stone fountain from the bedside table and hands it to Maya. "This is for you," she says. "Just make a wish." Maya closes her eyes and water bubbles from the top of the fountain.

Over the chattering fracas, no one hears her whisper, "I already got my wish."

2007

SONNY'S GIFTS

Choose your battles wisely, otherwise the minute you open
your mouth he will tune you out. - My father

Early in our relationship I realize that my Sonny is not one
for token demonstrations of his affections on Valentine's
Day, or any other day for that matter. Every year I
surprise him: a romantic night in a five-star hotel, tickets
to a Rolling Stone concert, a hot-air balloon ride over the
pyramids of Teotihuacan.

"I'm not going to be guilted by a consumer-crazed
society into giving you stuff on man-made holidays to
prove that I care about you." Sonny says when I mope
around the house. On Valentine's Day he adds historic
embellishment. "This started as an old Roman wine-
fueled fertility rite where men beat women with animal
skins. It's barbaric."

Holidays and birthdays come and go. Nothing. Then,
one Christmas, stressing from mountains of expectations

and too little time, I leave Sonny off my gift list. He never gives me anything; he won't mind.

Christmas morning, nothing left under the tree, the kids busy with their cache, Sonny says, "I guess I was bad this year. Didn't get anything."

"You never give me anything," I say. "I didn't think you'd care."

"But you're the gift giver," he says. "I don't know what to buy."

And then, over the years, gifts *happen*. Like in the deep of night, when Sonny knocks on doors looking for 15-year-old Roxy, lost in party frenzy; when he buys sweaters for our diva Chihuahua, and dresses him; or when he brings me tea and meals in bed for three weeks after a botched wisdom tooth extraction. I don't need chocolates and flowers.

2008

HUAMANTLA WITH CAMILLE

You have nothing to lose. - Anonymous

We're on our way to Huamantla, Tlaxcala, famous for
three things: an internationally acclaimed puppet museum;
an extraordinary town fair, which boasts a bull run
modeled after the one in Pamplona, Spain, and the sawdust
carpets, which blanket miles of the town's downtown
streets; and Danny's friend Beto. This year we'll be
attending, not only to partake in the town festivities, but
also to help Beto's dad, Alberto, celebrate his 50th birthday.

The whole town participates in the fair, and an entire
day is devoted to transforming ordinary sawdust into what
looks like plush carpeting with intricate, multicolored
designs. That night is known as The Night No One Sleeps,
and at midnight a statue of the Virgin Mary is carried
through the streets of downtown, the crowds destroying
the "rugs" as they follow behind. The procession

terminates at the church, where people wait in long lines that spill out into the front atrium and street. They're all anxious to enter the sacred space behind the altar in order to touch the blue satin cape of the same parading Virgin Mary, petitioning for better health, financial relief or cupid-like intervention. In the front patio, crowds of people jostle to view the plywood-size pictures of saints portrayed in colorful flowers.

PAINTED SAWDUST CARPET

My niece, Camille, Sonny and I will accompany Beto, who is nightclub-bouncer large. His round expressive eyes are put to good use on the stage, where he transforms into a wizard in my children's concert, The Apprentice and the Seven Tasks. Beto, without any acting experience, was drafted one day at the last minute when our professional wizard cancelled. He is so convincing in his role that children climb on the stage after performances to ask him if they can enroll in his School of Wizardry.

I assume Beto, who has traveled countless times to his father's hometown, knows the way, but how wrong I am!

"Since I always travel by bus, or someone else is driving, I never pay attention," he says.

"Maybe if you removed those damn earphones, or looked up once in a while from the video games, you'd learn your way around," I say. "You need to know where you're going!"

So, instead of forty minutes, the trip takes three pot-hole-riddled, traffic-jammed hours and by the time we arrive my patience is thin.

Alberto's birthday party boasts typical Mexican food: chicken enchiladas in green sauce, beef tacos and every adult beverage imaginable. Beto's dad and aunts treat us like royalty. I'm content to watch bashful Camille dance with a handful of Beto's handsome cousins until daybreak, when we're escorted to spacious bedrooms on the second floor of Beto's uncle's house   Down the hall is an indoor swimming pool and home movie theater that seats 25 people.

The real party begins the next day at a friend's second floor apartment which looks down on the street where the bulls will run. We begin the day right after breakfast with beer and margaritas. A four-foot high barrier of plywood lines the downtown streets for as far as the eye can see, and behind are makeshift bleachers. First, the parade passes with elaborate floats and musical groups. When they are safely behind protection, the bulls, are released in groups of three or four to chase the drunken revelers. Through the maze of streets they run, every so often a victim singled out, who usually jumps over the barricade. But sometimes the runner doesn't clear the barricade, he is thrown to the ground and mauled, the crowd wildly cheering.

The next day, we learn that only two lives are lost: a drunk, who fell asleep on the railroad track was hit by the train, and an alcohol-crazed teenager died from wounds inflicted by a scared, harassed bull.

On Monday we wake to Alberto honking the horn of a yellow Jeep he's borrowed from a friend.

"It's a great day for us to visit the Cantona Pyramids," he says. He and Sonny take the two front seats, Camille and I fold ourselves into the back.

The elements have worn away the original paint on most pyramids we've visited in Mexico, but here, protected by only a tin roof, we're delighted to see bright reds, oranges and blues, buried for centuries. Only a small area has been excavated, huge mounds of dirt hiding mysteries we won't be uncovering on this excursion. It's a treat to have the whole place to ourselves, except for a lone excavating archaeologist. A labyrinth of paths, bordered by the stone walls of ancient houses and mountains of rocks piled in pyramid formation, lead us finally to upper levels and an old ball-game court.

On the way to the nearby village, where we plan to spend the night, my cell phone rings with an alarming message from Gloria, the mother of Sara, my violin student: Please call as soon as possible. Again and again, I try to call, my phone losing its signal repeatedly. Finally Gloria answers.

"Don't worry about the mess or the blood all over your house," she says. " The girls are fine. We're all fine." Please don't say anything to anybody. I'll tell you all about what happened when I see you."

There's blood all over my house? I call her back.

"Don't worry, Maestra. We're all fine."

Gloria's husband, Jorge, was a private investigator. That morning, on the road north of my house, they'd found Jorge's truck with five bullet holes and blood stains. The family thought he'd been wounded or kidnapped. He'd been ambushed, and with two bullet wounds in his right shoulder, Jorge had jumped out of the truck and made for the woods, running south in the ravine until he found my house. No one was home, so he climbed in a window, found a first-aid kit in the bathroom, and bandaged his wounds, dripping blood as he went. As was our custom, we'd disconnected the house phones because lightning often blew them out. Jorge cut several lines, attaching them haphazardly, trying to get a phone line, but nothing worked. Finally, he drank a bottle of my best tequila, lay down on the living room couch and spotted the phone contact underneath the table. He called his family and they picked him up.

It's dark by the time we register at the hotel, not a soul is in sight. The Olympic-size swimming pool is inviting in the lingering heat, so Camille and I strip off our clothes and dive in. After we finish, we go back to the room. Alberto and Sonny take a turn, but they're not gone long.

"We've got to do something, quick!" Sonny says as he bursts into the room. "Look!"

"I'm itchy all over. I can't stand it," Alberto moans.

"It's some kind of allergic reaction," I say. "We've got

to get him to a hospital!"

Before our eyes, the skin over his entire body is wrinkling like a withered grape, his eyes disappear into his swelling face and his lips balloon. He's a monster.

It's midnight. We rush to the front desk to ask for the nearest hospital. But as soon as the owner of the hotel sees Alberto, he leads him to his car, rushing him to a nearby clinic. A few hours later, after an antihistamine injection and a saline drip, Alberto is still swollen, but out of danger. Alberto remembers that just before the swelling, he'd brushed some kind of insect from his neck. Spider? Scorpion?

"Never a dull moment in Mexico," Camille sighs.

2008

MY MOVIE STAR

The probability of a certain set of circumstances coming together in a meaningful (or tragic) way is so low that it cannot be considered mere coincidence. - V.C. King

It's late August, the classroom smells of rainy-season mold and locker-room sweat. I look around at fourteen classmates, half of them standing, others seated at desks in a square formation, a few cooling themselves with paper fans. Citlali, our writing teacher, suggests we go around the room and briefly introduce ourselves. After a girl in her early twenties gives her name and age, Citlali turns to me, peering over glasses. "This is an autobiography class," she whispers. "What can she write about?"

Next, it's Lucy's turn. She's an octogenarian immigrated from Europe as a young girl. Lucy doesn't say much at the first class but over the next ten weeks we're spellbound as she recounts her incredible life.

Lucy was born in 1928 in Genoa, Italy, to Swiss-German parents. Her father was Swiss ambassador in

Italy. A decade later, as WWII loomed, Italy's borders were closed, and Lucy's parents planned their escape. They could visit Switzerland but had to leave their ten-year-old daughter behind to guarantee their return. A few weeks later, Lucy and her Italian nanny (pretending to be Lucy's mother), escaped on a midnight train. Later that year the family moved to Mexico, never to look back.

This woman is walking history. I want to sit next to her, bring her water on a silver tray, fan her with a huge palm frond.

At the end of the year, Citlali announces that there will be a celebration of Lucy's life at the Teatro Morelos. I invite Sonny, who will go only if I treat him to a beer afterwards.

"It's a tribute to Lucy," I say. "She was a movie producer."

"Lucy Cabarga?" He's interested now.

"You know her?"

"When I was eighteen, I was in a movie she directed," he says. "The Cruelest Month. They filmed it at my mother's nightclub. I wonder what ever happened to that movie."

The auditorium of the largest theater in town is standing room only, the stage bursting with bright red, yellow and pink flower arrangements. Guest speakers take the podium to praise Lucy, at one time Mexico's leading woman producer of theater, television, and movies. "She produced over 52 films, some with American and European directors whom she convinced of the economic advantages of filming in Mexico."

I glance over at Lucy. She's beaming from a seat in the first row.

As I listen, I realize our paths have crossed before. Our history magically unfolds:

In 1983 Lucy co-produced the movie Under the Volcano and a call was made for extras. Lucy worked behind the scenes unbeknownst to me. My dad and Sonny jumped at the chance to work with Albert Finney in a film directed by John Huston. My heart pounds. We're part of this trailblazer's amazing story.

After the tribute is over and the standing ovation dies down, the lights dim, a screen drops from the ceiling and The Cruelest Month rolls. I gasp. There he is: young, handsome Sonny, dancing and smoking, his mother at his side!

ROXY, DAD, PETEY, ROBERT, SONNY, JUDITH, DOUG, ALICIA - FILMING <u>UNDER THE VOLCANO</u>

2008

THE FLOOD

It is a miracle that compassion and kindness exist at all in the world. - Me

The phone rings at sunrise, Sunday morning. A shaking female voice:

"I need to speak to Danny. Is he there? He was the DJ at my party last night here at my house. It rained and we gathered his speakers, but he needs to come get them. The Civil Engineers are coming and I'm not responsible if something gets stolen. How are the girls - your daughter and her friend?"

"My daughter and her friend?" I ask. "Roxy and Marcela? What are you talking about? The kids never came home last night!"

"Just tell Danny to come get his things." Click.

What a night to have lost power! Lightning blew out our landline and I couldn't charge my cell phone. This mysterious call came in just as I reconnected. Where are the kids? I know the house where Danny played. I pull

Sonny out of his early morning meditation, and we jump in the car.

The private home sits on the edge of a steep ravine, the uppermost floor, the garage, is level with the street. Doors hang wide open, not a soul in sight, no response when we yell a greeting, so we enter and start down the stairs on the left. Bedrooms are on the first floor, level with the garage, the living room-kitchen is the next level down, where the terrace and pool extend out over a 50 x 50-foot garden. Peering over the railing of the pool, to the garden below, I freeze. Broken glass, overturned metal tables and chairs, CDs litter the dance floor, deep in mud. A white canopy, which had sheltered the previous night's festivities, lies torn to shreds in filthy mounds. The silence is eerie, like the scene of a deadly car crash, sheets covering haphazardly thrown bodies. The 8-foot stone walls bordering the garden on the left and right are nothing but heaps of stone, exposing the lower neighbor's pool and debris-strewn yard on the right. A few waiters, dirt-streaked white shirts, limp red bow-ties, silently stumble about in the kitchen. They don't know where Danny is but point to the corner by the door. Danny's equipment is spattered in wet grass and dirt along with his $5,000, 4-set speaker system, disco lights, laptop computer, cables, microphones, CD jays, and console. My eyes sting and my throat tightens; it had taken Danny months of DJing all-night parties to pay for it all.

What happened? I'm paralyzed, everything moving around me in slow motion. Sonny, as if feeling my great sorrow, moves into action. He takes off his shoes, rolls up his jeans, and wades through the muck, gathering Danny's CDs, sparkling in the early rays of sunrise. He gathers together the Timbiriche and giant shark costumes the guests had danced in, just a few hours earlier. But where are the kids? It's not like Danny to just walk away from his stuff.

I call Pete. "Where have you been all night?" he says. "Why didn't you answer your phone?" Pete explains that Danny, Roxy and her friend Marcela were here last night when the retaining walls gave way and the place flooded. "Marcela's Achilles' heel was severed to the bone," he says. "Roxy and Danny went to the Red Cross Hospital in the ambulance with her. The surgery took five hours and Danny paid the bills with all the money he earned last night. They're here at my house now. Stay where you are. I'll be right over."

A disheveled woman in a pink sweat-suit, hair a tangled mess, eye-make-up streaks half-way down her cheeks, approaches as I hang up the phone. She's the owner of the house, the woman who called earlier.

"I'm a nervous wreck," she repeats, over and over, as if her mind has been swept away by the floodwaters.

"Marcela had surgery," I say. "Maybe we can split the hospital bill. She was visiting my daughter and I feel responsible. It's the right thing to do. "

"Yes, I have your phone number, I'll call you. I need to go now."

Pete arrives and fills us in. An old mattress, plastic bottles and tree limbs dammed up the river behind the garden wall. Roxy and Marcela had just finished a fire dance around midnight, when Danny noticed the water seeping through the wall. He asked the hostess if he could pack up.

"There are still a few guests and your time's not up.

You stay right where you are," she said, as she and most of her guests moved to the upper levels of the house, out of the rain.

When the wall collapsed, an eight-foot wave came crashing in, sweeping Roxy and Marcela through a glass door, down a 20-foot hallway and into a bathroom. The water filled the room, hallway, and garden, by now a churning whirlpool. Roxy swam to the top of the water-filled chamber, found no air, then pounded the walls desperate for an opening to swim out of the blackness. They were trapped.

Meanwhile, Danny and Willy, Danny's assistant, were dragged up the outside stairway leading to the house. Danny had seen Roxy and Marcela sucked into the hallway and was about to swim into the tunnel, when the lower garden wall broke, releasing the water into the property below and pulling the kids from a watery grave.

The same night, two policemen are washed away while trying to dislodge a Volkswagen Beetle from the water raging half a mile down the same ravine. One is found a few days later under a pile of rock and rubble. The other vanishes. We have been spared.

At the Red Cross Hospital, the doctors take one look at Marcela and make an emergency, middle-of-the-night call to a surgeon who specializes in tendons. Learning that Marcela is from Ciudad Acapulco, Tamaulipas, 1,000 kilometers from home, the doctor charges $300 US (3,000 pesos) instead of his normal fee of $2,000 US (20,000 pesos).

Danny has another DJ job in just two days! I call Javier, a friend in the DJ business, to see about renting equipment. After I explain the tragedy, he is encouraging:

"Don't worry, I'll do everything to get him through this. I'll lend him my best equipment; a light and sound show like nothing seen before. And I'm not charging a dime."

Sonny and I spend the following week opening speakers and washing Danny's equipment. Danny paces through the house, retelling what happened, unable to focus enough to help us in the clean-up.

At the next job with my string quartet, I tell Jose, the wedding coordinator, about the flood and Danny's soggy equipment.

"Why didn't you tell me?" he says. "I studied electrical engineering. I'd be glad to show you how to clean them up."

Marcela, four months and four operations later, including a skin graft from her thigh, begins to walk. Most of the equipment was saved. The cell phones and scanner lights are ruined as is the shark costume, who, everyone jokes, was the only one who enjoyed the flood.

Several times Danny tries to call the owner of the house, but she's never available. She never calls about Marcela's hospital bills as promised, or even to inquire if Marcela can walk; she's not interested to know if Danny's equipment is salvaged. Because of her arrogance and poor judgment, my kids and their friends almost lost their lives. One friend suggests we hire a lawyer. Danny wants what's fair, but after three years in the courts, we lose the case. Apparently, a deal was made between the lawyers on both sides, Danny and Marcela's losses not even considered in the negotiations.   I was hoping for a bit of integrity, if not from the legal system, from the woman who almost drowned our kids.

Now, all of us have a greater respect for Tlaloc, the Aztec god of rain and fertility, who demanded child sacrifices. We're grateful our children were spared.

2008

WE WORK FOR GOD

Never put yourself in a position to be made an example of.
- Gary Hopkins

Whenever anyone asks Sonny what we do for a living, he smiles and says, "We work for God!" That's partly true, I suppose. Our quartet plays for spiritual ceremonies that celebrate life milestones, like *quince años,* weddings and funerals. It's lucrative work and even more so for the Catholic church.

One couple asks if we can lower our fee, complaining that they already paid $1,500 dollars to rent the cathedral for an hour and the priest charged an additional $1,000.

Considering the expense of these rites, I'm aghast at one wedding when, just as the groom fumbles with a gold band, a hunchbacked crone tugs at my sleeve.

"I'm collecting the fee for the electricity," she says.

"We're only using a tiny bit for the electric piano," I whisper.

"And the lights," she says, pointing to the glistening

chandelier over the altar. "Fifty pesos ($5.00 dollars) per person."

"You need to wait until he's done," I say, nodding at the priest. "We can't ask now!"

The woman slinks away. snaking her way through the perfumed-chiffon packed pews, and never returns.

At one wedding, we arrive at the venue to find a mandolin, a guitar, a guitarron (a hand-held bass) and a keyboard, an *estudiantina,* in our space, setting up equipment.

"The bride and her mother hired us," I say to the man tuning his guitar.

He looks up and shakes his head. "We're playing this one."

I hover behind the group, set up at the end of the parents' row. They begin a loud, out-of-tune folk version of the Mendelssohn Wedding March. The groom and his entourage all stare in horror as they pass. The flustered bride, looking our way, catches a heel on her gown and trips. Baffled as she is, I shrug and gesture towards the musicians.

The mass continues, the guests, turning towards the mystery group at every dissonant intervention, as if in morbid disbelief. The final blessing conferred, the bride and groom make a dash for the reception, as shrieking mothers storm us.

"Can't you play even one piece right? It was horrible! An abomination!"

"You hired two groups!" I say.

"No! I hired you!" one screams, pointing at me.

"They wouldn't let us play," I say.

Shaking heads and mumbling, they stomp off behind the last of the guests and scattered white programs.

The priest, drawn by the commotion, rushes over. "What's going on?"

"They didn't like the music!" guitar man says. "They said we were awful."

"How ungrateful," the priest says. "They don't appreciate my gift. I haven't signed any documents yet. Maybe I'll just annul this marriage!"

At another wedding, the priest arrives an hour late. We've been ready for two hours. As he sets up his table with a white tablecloth, a silver grail, and wafers, I greet him.

"We're all running late," I say. "We have another mass to play after this one."

He takes a vial of water from his backpack and pours. I don't exist.

The priest welcomes the bride and groom at the altar and then says, "The musicians have another commitment. I say they should leave now!" And he motions with his hand for us to be gone.

During his sermon the priest garbles on and on, guests yawn and twitch. And so, just before communion, the sand empties from the hourglass, we pack up and tiptoe out. The priest prattles on.

Monday morning, before my coffee percolates, the phone rings. It's the bride's mother. "You ruined my daughter's wedding!" she says. "I want my money back!"

"We complied with the contract," I say. "We arrived half an hour early and even stayed an extra hour because the priest was late."

"He was late because of some unforeseen problem."

"He had another mass," I say. "In Cuernavaca. An hour away. He ruined your wedding. Tell him you want a refund."

"I can't say that to a priest," she says. "That would be sacrilegious."

The priest at the Guadalupe Church wears a jewel encrusted crown and a red velvet floor-length cape and bears a polished gold scepter. A Santa-sized belly protrudes from his robe and his cheeks are speckled in pock marks.

CAMERATA DE ORO – HACIENDA DE CORTÉS

There are never rehearsals for these life milestones, so, on arrival, we always ask the man in charge to approve the couple's musical selections. Every priest has a different criterion for what's appropriate during the hour of their reign.

"Buenos días," I say, handing his majesty the list.

He yanks the paper from my hand and throws it to the floor, as if it's Martin Luther's Thesis. "This is not a concert!" he says. "You'll play only the marches. That's all I'll allow!"

The unsuspecting bride and groom enter and stand waiting, while the priest takes his place on the throne, stares into space, chin regally high, and then glares at us. "I want the Gloria! Now! Play it!"

We scramble to find the page in our books. The couple at the altar shake their heads as we comply with his whimsical requests throughout the mass, disregarding their harmonious dreams.

Yes, we try to work for God, try to let the spirit move during these sacred ceremonies, but usually the priest thwarts any inkling of Divine Manifestation.

2009

SOFI AND HER KITS

All my girls will get a university education. That way they
won't have to put up with an abusive situation.
– My mother

The village knows of our work with the youth orchestra,
even Valeria's sixth-grade teacher. She calls to ask if I
can help train selected students in perfecting the Mexican
national anthem. Valeria is a promising violin student, and
I worry about her as I do about all the girls I teach.
Already three have dropped out of orchestra because of
teenage pregnancies.

    The following Tuesday I set up my keyboard in a
chilly, cinderblock classroom with desks pushed up
against the far wall. Twenty-five fifth and sixth grade girls
in uniforms file in and form rows. A cloud of perfume,
hairspray and sweat settles around them. Their uniforms
of blue-plaid skirts and green sweaters, white bobby socks
and black polished shoes remind me of army-style

discipline. They stand at attention, eyes fixed on the empty blackboard. I greet them and nod to Valeria, in the first row.

"It's great to be here," I say. "A little strange that only girls will perform in the national anthem competition."

No one answers; the room is still, except for birdsong from the window ledge outside.

Trying to get them to relax, I say, "What would you like to be when you grow up, if you could be anything?"

Silence. I prompt: "A judge? A pilot? A teacher?"

Again, no one volunteers.

"Come on," I say. "Someone say something."

A collective sigh and then, one after another, giggles, each one confirming, "A housewife, Miss. We want to be housewives."

"You can have a career and be housewives," I say. "I do both."

They smile and shake their heads, resigned to the fate of village women.

In orchestra class I tell everyone, "You can be whatever you want to be, even you girls." And at home I start work on my project.

Some of the older students don't know what a menstrual cycle is or how a baby is conceived. They need information. I imagine a mini booklet describing the changes to expect at puberty and a little gift bag for girls with soaps, body cream, Kotex and a razor.

First, I hire a well-known children's book illustrator to design the bi-lingual booklet where a hip, teenage, multi-racial Sofi explains it all. I find a printer in Mexico City and order 3,000 copies of the booklet, then buy as many hotel-size products.

And then come the sales: A cement company, *Cementos Moctezuma*, donates 500 kits to teens in the local village, where the company is tearing up the mountain to extract raw materials.

A male friend, Armando, teaches Life Skills at a low-income junior high. One of his students, 14-year-old Leonora, has been absent a lot. When she is in class, she passes the time bent over her desk, her long, black hair hiding her face. On the way out of class one day she hands my friend a scrap of paper from her dad: PLEASE TEACH LEONORA ABOUT MENSTRUATION.

"This girl has six brothers and lives with her father. Now they want me to teach her about menstruation. I need help," he says, and buys a kit for Leonora.

The next time I see Armando, he tells me, "Leonora is a changed person. She beams."

Another 11-year-old girl runs away from home. The girl is bleeding and thinks her mother will punish her for some wrongdoing. The mother needs to be disciplined for not giving her daughter essential information.

"I didn't know how to tell her," she says, wringing her hands. "This kit will help a lot."

All of this is inspiring, yet I feel the most joy when eager 10-year-old girls in the youth orchestra, receive their long-awaited, informative kits.

Over the years, more budding musicians drop out of the orchestra to take care of babies. I write another bi-lingual booklet, where Sofi, and her invented boyfriend, David, explain contraceptives and STDs. This one comes with a condom.

"If we give them a condom, the first thing they'll want

to do is go out and have sex," the mother of cellist Violeta, says, when I offer the booklet. A year later, without a booklet or a condom, 16-year-old Violeta drops out of school and orchestra.

"I wanted to see what it felt like to have a baby," Violeta says, visiting an orchestra rehearsal with her baby screaming in arms. "It's a lot of work. You were right to tell us to wait."

Now I need to make a kit for new Moms. One that says how they need to speak to their girls, how to encourage their daughters to love themselves, to be independent and to realize their dreams.

And then there's menopause...

Over the years, many of the girls do in fact study careers, a few are even professional musicians. I don't know if it was the Sofi Kits or it was watching their peers roaming the village, looking for work, babies strapped on their backs, that convinced them to wait. But I'm glad they did.

2009

MONDAY MADNESS

"Cuando te toca, aunque te quites, y cuando no te toca, aunque te pongas." When it's your time, it doesn't matter what you do to avoid it, and if it's not your time, you won't die no matter what you do. - Mexican Proverb

A day has to be really wacky to stand out in Mexico, where most days unfold with myriad surprises. April 29th, 2009 is such a day.

The constant ringing of the phone shakes me awake. It's Eduardo's mother. He's a struggling trumpet player in the youth orchestra in Huitzilac.

"Eduardo's father is dead," she says. "It's the swine flu. The government has closed all the schools and parents are freaking out. We have to cancel orchestra rehearsal."

Eduardo's father was only 38.

At eleven o'clock I'm working at my desk when the windows and the glasses in the cupboard begin to rattle, the hanging lamps swing. I run out of the house to find the giant pines and oaks full-hurricane flailing, but there's no wind. I know I'm safe: there are no power lines or buildings to electrocute or crush me, and no danger of gas or water lines breaking. After the trees stop shaking, I step back inside and check the walls and beams. No cracks or broken windows, even though the news reports 5.6 on the Richter scale.

At three that afternoon, I take the overgrown path out to the garden to hang clothes to dry. Suddenly, there's rustling in the leaves a few feet ahead. Probably birds scratching for food, I think as I approach. But no, there she waits, a tight coil, head bobbing. I know she'll strike only as a last resort, since she'll be left defenseless after injecting her venom. I live so far away from the nearest hospital that I won't survive a rattlesnake bite. I back up in slow motion and the snake slithers away.

The most remarkable event occurs that evening. At exactly seven on that extraordinary Monday, I pull up to the house of my 11-year-old violin and English student. It's drizzling and I huddle under the roof at the door and pull the metal chain to ring the bell.

I turn around, look up into the metal-grey sky above the pine forest across the street, and sigh with gratitude. What a paradise! Then, a deafening explosion of white light. I examine my hands. Am I still alive?

The door opens and Ceci's grandmother, Conchita, greets me, pale and trembling.

"I can't believe you're alive!" she says. "I thought the lightning had taken you!"

I *am* lucky to be alive, I think, as we gaze at flames whipping the upper branches of the 60-foot pine tree. Lightning struck the tree and jumped into a telephone cable running perpendicular to the tree, blowing out service at every home along its path. A cable saved my life!

Then, a dramatic outpouring of Conchita's experience:

"Years ago, a friend and I were walking in an open field. It was overcast, but not a drop of rain. Then, out of nowhere, lightning struck, sent us flying. I stood up, called out to my friend, but she didn't move. She was about twenty feet away and didn't respond when I shook her. When the police came, they took me to jail. Thought I'd killed her, I guess. They let me go after the autopsy. It was horrible."

I call Sonny and recount my lucky day. "Get back to bed," he says. "And start over."

2009

THE PIJIMENTE VIOLIN

Nothing in my life is a coincidence. -Kami Garcia

The summer of 2009 I look forward to a relaxed two-week visit with my brother Henry and his family in Michigan, but Sonny has other plans for me. He wants me to sell a violin because the repairs it requires are beyond his expertise.

It's a mystery how this 18th century French violin found its way to a monastery in the mountains south of Mexico City. But just as baffling is how Sonny is persuaded, like Jack and the famous beans, to trade his beloved Nissan truck for this instrument.

The three-inch peg inside, under the bridge, supports the pressure of the strings and carries sound from the top to the back of the violin. In prosaic English it's called a sound post, but the Romance languages consider it el alma (the soul). Where this violin's sound post presses against the back, a hairline fissure bleeds out inches into the wood, rendering it basically worthless.

Henry lives twenty minutes from one of the largest mail-order retailers of string instruments in the country.

My hand shakes as I dial the number to the shop. String instrument appraisers are sharks, shaming owners into thinking their instruments are worthless, then purchasing them for pennies on their resale dollars.

"Could I make an appointment for a violin appraisal?" I say.

"We get calls from people all the time who think they've found a priceless Stradivarius in grandma's attic. Don't want to disappoint you, but that's rare."

"Please, just take a look," I say. "I'm a violinist and I've come a long way. From Mexico."

"It'll be forty dollars for a verbal appraisal and eighty for a written. Noon tomorrow."

That night I toss and turn and pray for a miracle. It's the split in the wood that I worry about. And why is it my problem? Dealing with damaged violins or relationships seems to always fall on me. Like when our marriage cracked when Sonny thought he might prefer another wife. I managed to patch that up. And that was much more challenging than this instrument's hairline fracture.

The next day, my brother lends me his car with GPS, and I arrive five minutes before my appointment. The bell on the door tinkles, and I'm inside a shop the size of a fast-food restaurant, except here, the air smells of wood and rosin. Cellos, violas and violins hang from the ceiling, sheet music bulges from racks. I'm ushered down a hall and into a room with hundreds of oversized post-office boxes, a violin scroll peeking from each. In the center, an operating-room size lamp hangs over a long, waist-high wooden table. Through a plate-glass window on the far wall I can see several master healers hunched over their centuries-old patients.

A young man, about my son's age, greets me. Looking through the f-holes into the body he reads the labels with dates of prior repairs: 1874 by Frank Grey, 1917 by Mr. Lindholm, both from St. Louis, Missouri. Burned on the back, in barely discernible letters is "F. Pijemente, a Paris." Patching changes an instrument, its exquisite voice never to sing as the master luthier intended.

In silence, the young man turns the violin over and over on the table, like a doctor, his gaze exploring, searching for defects. I hold my breath.

Finally, he speaks, but not about the violin. "You say you're from Mexico. I lived in Mexico when I was young. 1977 to 1979."

"I was there then," I say. "Where?"

"My father, Thomas, played viola in an orchestra in Toluca."

"You must be Boris, then!" I say, doing the math in my head. "You and your brother used to eat quesadillas in my kitchen while your mom and I planned for my new baby."

"I've known you for thirty years," Boris says, shaking his head. Whether it's the personal connection or he simply sees its value, he says, "I could send this violin with our December lot to Tarisios in New York City. They'll auction it as an interesting and repairable instrument.'"

Boris does as promised and ships the Pijemente to Tarisios. We watch the online auction and it sells for $1,500 dollars.

Someone has faith that this instrument is repairable, that it will someday sing again. I believe that I will, also.

2009

THE POND

You have to do something three times to get it right.
- My father.

The pond is my dream, and Sonny makes it clear that he's not interested. "Build it if you want," he says. "But it's your project." I need to hire Felipe, the overseer, buy cement and sand, and feed the workers on the day they pour.

At ten in the morning the sand arrives. "Where do I dump?" the driver yells.

He and his helper blow cigarette smoke from the cab while I look for a place to unload. Suddenly Felipe appears, bloodshot eyes, beaming grin. I run for Sonny.

"I'm not dealing with him if he's drunk," Sonny says.

"Fine," I say, racing back to the truck. "Felipe, how are you going to make my pond if you're drunk?" I ask.

"Very, very well. Like magic," he says, spit flying, bursts of laughter. He stumbles onto the front bumper and the men in the cab laugh and honk the horn.

"Dump it over behind the little house," I say. "Where

it's easy to get to."

The next day Felipe begins construction alone, digging a hole the size of an Olympic swimming pool. At the end of the week, he lays the rebar and it's ready for cement.

"It's the custom for the patron to feed us lunch the day we pour," Felipe says, wiping dirt from his pants. "There'll be ten of us. Is that going to be a problem?"

"Can your wife Minerva make lunch?" I say. "I don't know what you like."

Yes, she can. I give Felipe some cash for rice, beans, chicken and tortillas. Then, aiming to establish boundaries, I add, "Sonny says don't come to work drunk."

"We don't drink on the job," he says, smiling.

Fifteen men with shovels and picks rattle us awake at daybreak. Felipe is jumpy. Maybe the rumors are true that he likes cocaine. He assigns jobs: some will gather and pour the sand and gravel, a few will haul water, and the rest, in a circle, will mix.

I've visited every do-it-yourself pond-site on the internet. I know the proportions: three parts gravel, two parts sand, and one-part cement. They're doing it all wrong!

"Felipe, you're putting in too much cement," I say.

"Those assholes don't know what they're talking about," Felipe snaps. "The damn architects demand that we do things a certain way and when they don't turn out right, they blame us. I say let them all go to hell, those fucking faggots."

Shovels stop. Silence. All eyes are on me. I turn and walk back to the house.

"Are you crazy?" Sonny says after I tell him. "You can't go out there and tell him how to do things in front of his men. You're a woman!"

"But you refuse to talk to him!"

"You wanted a pond and you hired Felipe. Now finish what you started."

It's definitely not the time to enlighten Felipe about women's strides in the 21st century. I've dreamed about this pond for too long. I bite my tongue.

8:30 A.M. Felipe is knocking again. "My crew is leaving."

"What is it now?"

"They're thirsty. They want their sodas."

I give Felipe's son $100 pesos and send him to the store for 10 bottles of sugar fix.

THE POND

Later, from my window, I see most of the guys leaning on their shovels chatting, only a few at work. I call Felipe to the house. "Why did you hire so many men if only a few are working?"

"Four of them are supervisors," he says, eyeing his dirt-encrusted fingernails. "We need more cement. Only half the pond is poured and we're out."

That doesn't surprise me.

I convince Sonny to drive to the village for twenty-five more bags. A few hours later the job is done and it's time for lunch.

Felipe's wife has brought the food from home in big clay pots. The men plop down on inverted paint buckets around an open-air fire, where Minerva pats out tortillas, cooking them on a round clay *comal,* a round fire-resistant plate. Shoving tacos into his mouth, Felipe shoots insults at his wife: "This food is bland- absolutely no flavor. It needs chili peppers. And salt."

I was right about the proportions. During the seven-month dry spells the water recedes, seeping away like youthful expectations. And when the water level is at its lowest, Sonny strolls out to the pond and sits, by the hour, making repairs his own way.

2010

LOVE AND SEBASTIAN

You cannot do a kindness too soon because you never know how soon it will be too late. - Ralph Waldo Emerson

Rapid banging wakes me. It's sunrise and Sofía, our 44-year-old neighbor, is at the door. "He's gone!" she says, pulling at her wet hair, pacing. "I can't find Sebastian."

"Oh God," I say. "The pond."

"I looked there," she says, heaving. "I even ran home to check. He's nowhere."

"Let me wake Sonny. He can help us look."

"I told her not to come around anymore," Sonny says, buttoning his pants, running his hand through his hair. "She's always taking stuff without asking: milk, firewood, Wi-Fi."

"We need to find him," I say. "Hurry."

"She never watches that baby," he says. "I knew this would happen."

"You've got to dredge the pond," I say. "I can't live through another drowning."

279

On the terrace, sleep-groggy Sonny asks, "How long has he been missing?"

"Half an hour," Sofía says, choking. "I was checking emails, and he disappeared.

Sonny shakes his head. "Even if we find him..."

"Please Sonny," I say. "Just go in. Sofía, let's circle the property."

Sonny strips and jumps into the icy water, combing through schools of panicked goldfish and thick cattails. We run through the forest yelling Sebastian's name, the dogs barking. Nothing.

"He cries when you leave the room," I say. "This is so unlike him. I'll run to the road."

Half-way to the highway I meet a rusted green Volkswagen beetle. It coughs a cloud of gasoline, lurches and dies. An old man is at the wheel, two-year-old Sebastian, golden curls bobbing, smiles and waves from the back seat.

"Is he yours?" the man asks. "He was running down my road towards the village."

"Sofía, come!" I yell. "He must've crawled out through the hole the dogs dug under the fence."

"I was taking him to city hall, but remembered *gueros,* blondies, lived on this road."

Sofía opens the door and grabs Sebastian, crying kisses into his curls.

"You need to watch your son," the old man says to Sofía. "He could've been kidnapped."

Sonny, speckled in mud and dead leaves, pulls himself from the pond. "What I do for you, Laurie," his blue lips whisper.

2010

MY PIANO

It's an ill wind that blows no good. - John Heywood

One was reddish-brown and the other black. My dad had hauled in two ancient baby grand pianos advertised for free and placed them curve to curve in our sun porch music room, like lovers embracing. Big pianos were a cumbersome burden for people without the love of music in their hearts.

The room was waist-high-to-ceiling windows, especially lovely when the setting sun warmed with golden-red hues. I dreamed of four-hand piano duets with my siblings, but the pianos were never tuned to the same pitch. No one seemed to care except me. I longed for a new piano, unaware that I'd be waiting fifty years.

It was 2010 and Sonny and I taught orchestra for a government sponsored program in Mexico. For nine months we hadn't seen a paycheck, and neither had over one hundred other teachers. We knew that when the money *did* arrive, we'd have to pay a third in taxes if we didn't buy something related to our work. Something big. Something expensive. A piano! But not just any piano. We wanted a baby grand, queen of pianos.

We scour Mexico City looking for the best deal and find that two major music stores are out of business. Playing a musical instrument has gone the way of the horse and buggy and drive-in movie theaters. Then, on the third floor, in a mall department store, tucked into an obscure corner, we find a baby grand piano surrounded by five electronic keyboards. I run my fingers lightly over the the keys.

"Are you in a hurry to buy a piano?" a young salesman behind me asks.

"It has to be before the end of the year," I say.

"If you can wait two weeks, we'll be having our 'midnight madness' sale where everything is 20% off," he says. "Pianos included. And we give you 100 store coins for every 1,000 pesos you spend. You cash the coins in for merchandise." He shows us a glossy brochure with televisions, blenders, computers, iPads, cameras, printers, pots and pans, and wine. How can we refuse?

Trusting that we'll see our checks before the year's end, we hand over $7,000 US in cash and put another $6,000 on a credit card. The clerk hands us two bottles of wine, a USB flash drive, a printer, and an iPad. "Go celebrate," he says. "You'll see your piano in three weeks."

The year is almost over, and we sweat but finally, December 29th, the government deposits nine months of classes. Liquidating the credit card is easy, but the piano delivery is as challenging as a breech birth.

Three weeks later, a moving truck rumbles up our dirt

road, but halfway, an overhanging limb blocks the road. Three men jump down from the cab. One pulls open the back door and two climb in. After rummaging around, they throw a dolly down to the third and slide a huge cardboard box to the edge. They know nothing about moving a two-ton instrument.

"Hold on a minute," Sonny says. "I'll run and get my chain saw."

"We don't have time for that," dolly man says, pointing to the inside of the truck.. "We've got to deliver these mattresses."

"If you wait, I'll go get more people to help carry the piano," Sonny says. "It's too heavy for you three."

"There were eight of us guys at the warehouse to put the piano on the truck," dolly man says. "But they only assigned three of us for the delivery. Come on, let's have the piano."

"You're going to get hurt." Sonny says. He runs to get the chainsaw as I watch two men drop the box onto the dolly. My heart aches. Then, the three men push and pull the dolly up the bumpy, rocky driveway. A step looms to the terrace. Oh God, now what?

"Sonny, they're ruining the piano," I say.

"Wait," he says, looking at the men. "There's no way you're going to lift it." He runs behind the house and returns with two thick ropes. Two men on each side, including Sonny, sling the rope over their backs, slip it under the box and lift the piano up onto the terrace. Then, they drag the box across to the door, knocking off the square metal shock absorbers. My mouth drops open as they slide the monster down three more clay-tile steps into our living room.

"Don't open the box," one of the men says. "Experts from Yamaha will be out in a few days to set it up."

"You tore the box to shreds when you dragged it," I say.

"That doesn't matter," he says, as he walks outside. "Let's go boys." He clears his throat and spits in the driveway, and the three jog off leaving a cloud of dust behind.

Five experts arrive a week later to assemble the piano. "You shouldn't have accepted the merchandise in this condition," one man says, shaking his head at the torn box. "Let's see what we've got here."

Holding my breath, I watch as they open the box with screwdrivers and unveil the shining black beauty. They screw in the legs, and finally, turn the piano upright. My heart is pounding, fingers twitching to play, but I notice a big scratch the length of one side and a corner of wood is missing. The men stare at the damage. One takes out his phone and snaps pictures. "We need to report this," he says.

The action is also damaged. Three times the men withdraw, insert, and try to line up the keyboard with the hammers, but the keys take too long to return to position. I shake my head and sigh, tears welling.

"Since it's the Christmas holidays, we won't be able to send anyone out for a few weeks to touch up the wood and tune it," one of the men says.

"I want another one," I say. "We bought a new piano and I expect it to be perfect. Would you buy a brand-new car with a scratch down the side and part of the bumper missing? With a transmission that doesn't work? Would you accept it?"

The men examine their shoes, balance from one foot to the other. "No," one says, shaking his head. "You're right. We'll let the boss know."

Month after month I call the store, but the answer is always the same: "We´ve searched all over Mexico, but your model is unavailable."

I won't give up and call every other day. Then, one day, they call me.

"We found you a piano. Will you be home tomorrow?"

"Where did you find it?" I say.

"The truth is, the moving company's insurance finally agreed to pay."

Sonny cuts the culprit limb, and the next day eight bodyguards arrive with the precious cargo. They install it with the reverence and care it deserves. As they load the damaged piano into the truck, a chill runs down my spine. "What will they do with that one?"

"They'll try to fix it," one man says. "But who knows, it might end up in a display case."

"What a waste."

When they're done Sonny invites the bodyguards to the local village to celebrate with tacos and beer. I stay behind, and, in the silence, alone with this shining beauty, I stare. Then, I walk towards my gift, heart pounding, and sit on the pristine, black leather bench. And I play and I play and I play and when I finish, I lean my head on the shining finish and I cry.

2011

CHURCH PREDICAMENTS

The church has always been willing to swap off treasure in heaven for cash down. - Robert C. Ingersoll

From the start, I have a bad feeling about this wedding. The bride wants her best friend, Mary Lou, to sing the Ave Maria. Family and friends participating in the ceremony can add a lovely touch, but on more than one occasion a tone-deaf relative has crashed the party. You wouldn't let cousin Leonard operate on your gall bladder just because he knows how to carve up a turkey, would you? But Nurse Mary Lou sings once a month at the Noteworthy Girls Chorus, so they think she's qualified.

Weeks before the wedding the telephone doesn't stop ringing. Mary Lou wants to rehearse.

"We've played these tunes hundreds of times," I say. "We can run through your Ave Maria just before the mass."

"I can't believe you're so uncooperative," she says, and hangs up.

As usual, the day of the wedding I arrive an hour early at the church, and the sacristan makes us wait fifteen minutes before he leads us up the wide stone steps to unlock the ten-foot 16th century weathered wooden door. The loft smells damp and musty, eight long wooden benches line up in single file facing the waist-high splintered wooden banister. The altar is a football field length away. The Cuernavaca Cathedral is over 500 years old and whitewashing has been carefully removed in patches to reveal a 17th century narrative mural.

Jose unpacks his violin and Keiko sets up her keyboard, while I play my violin for Mary Lou's coveted rehearsal, checking tempos and dynamics. Unlike her abrasive telephone personality, she's good-natured and her satiny smooth voice surprises us.

We can see the bridal party gathering outside the side door just below the loft.

"Sonny, you'd better go back down to the office and remind the sacristan to turn on the electricity," I say. "We have no speakers, no organ!"

Five minutes later Sonny's back, waving a paper. "I had to pay him 100 pesos ($10.00 USD) to flip the switch on. Here's a copy of the contract the bride and groom signed. It says right here: 'The donation to the church is 6,000 pesos ($600.00 USD) for an hour mass and an additional fee if the musicians use electricity.'"

"But my friend paid 10,000 pesos for this mass!" Mary Lou says.

Keiko connects her piano and speaker to the only outlet she can find and clicks it on. The power strip explodes. Keiko gasps. Smoke and the smell of burning plastic fill the air.

The wedding coordinator looks up from the doorway below and nods, our signal to begin. Keiko fiddles with the equipment but the speaker is dead. Mary Lou shakes her head and stares at the keyboard.

"Sonny, please go back down to the office and tell them what happened!" I say.

The wedding planner is waving as if she's trying to stop a runaway locomotive bearing down on the cathedral. "Start the wedding march now," she mouths. We do our best to fill the cavernous cathedral with Mendelssohn's Wedding March but two violins and a keyboard without amplification fall short. Playing from memory, I look down and see the mother of the bride throw up her arms and roll her eyes as she files in.

Sometime between the offertory and the communion Sonny's back with the sacristan, who wriggles the cable into different contacts on the power strip. Finally, the speaker crackles to life.

"Who's in charge here?" I say. "I want a new power strip and my 100 pesos."

"You plugged into the wrong outlet," he says. "We're not responsible," and leaves.

Mary Lou is halfway through the Ave Maria when the sacristan stomps back, bearing the goods I requested. He offers the power-chord, but I don't stop playing until the communion is over.

"I've done what you asked," he says. "Are you happy?"

"This cathedral could use a 20th century Martin Luther to tack another list on the door."

The sacristan bristles and scurries away.

Mary Lou shakes her head as she gathers up her music. "The bride is going to hear about this! A mess! And it wasn't because we didn't rehearse enough!"

We've pulled it off, I think.

Two weeks later, I'm back at the cathedral with the Morelos Chamber Orchestra to perform The Seven Last Words of Christ by Joseph Haydn. The orchestra is in front of the altar with the 15-voice choir behind us. During the rehearsal I look up from my stand to see the sacristan, from the explosion-in-the-loft incident, in the first pew watching me.

The concert is applauded by an overflow crowd and the sacristan's wicked stare is far from my mind as Sonny and I leave the cathedral. Walking the dimly lit stone path through the flower garden, someone runs up from behind: a tall, light-haired man, in fine-tailored casual dress.

"You both played very beautifully," he says. "I want to congratulate you."

"Thank you," I say. "And who are you?"

"I'm the main priest of this cathedral," he says. "You played here a couple of weeks ago in a wedding. The music tonight was beautiful, but you have an ugly filthy mouth."

"I've never seen you in my life. What did I say?"

"That all priests are corrupt," he hisses.

"I did not. But I did say that it's so sad that the church is so materialistic!"

"We gave you your money back," he says. "You have no idea how much it costs to run this cathedral."

"I don't agree with everything she says," Sonny blurts.

What? Sonny's not even Catholic! I feel betrayed.

The priest turns to go but hesitates: "And I know good and well who Martin Luther is!" Finally, the real reason he's attacking me.

"You have no right to judge," Sonny scolds, after the priest leaves.

"I'm not judging," I say. "I'm angry that they've lost sight of what Jesus is all about. They've buried him under fees and regulations. My Grandma Rosie gave money to the church for years to keep her dead brother out of hell. Martin Luther complained about indulgences over 500 years ago. It's still going on!"

"You better watch it" Sonny says. "You're going up against the Catholic Church and you know that people who disagree with them sometimes disappear."

We walk in silence across the street to Marco Polo's Italian Restaurant.

"There's a part of you that I really hate," Sonny says after we order. "You think you're always right."

"Oh yeah?" I snap "Really? Is that what you think?" I grab my purse and my violin and dash down the stairs, a blur of people and cars, and then I spy a taxi at a traffic light. Sonny is following me. I slide into the back seat, but Sonny grabs the door. What will he say? Will he apologize? The driver and I wait to hear, breathless.

"What should I do with the food you ordered?" he asks.

"I don't care what you do with it," I say, slamming the door shut.

Tears burn my eyes, I'm furious. We drive around for 15 minutes because I haven't given the driver a destination and he doesn't ask. Spying a hotel, I ask him to drop me there. *"Que te vaya bien,"* Hope it goes well, he says gently; a supporting actor, whose bit part is only 15 minutes, but so vital.

I rip my long black dress as I stumble up the stairs and into the lobby.

"Are you alone?" the clerk asks, eyeing my violin and my mascara-smeared face.

"Yes, very," I say, and book a room.

A young boy escorts me to my room where I drop onto the bed. More tears.

Sonny calls. Three times. He's worried I need food.

I'm not going to allow the church to interfere in my marriage, I think, and on the fourth call I give him the name of the hotel.

"I'm sorry I didn't stand up for you," Sonny says when I open the door.

I'm looking forward to a healing chat, but I guess he thinks his apology is enough, because he flops onto the bed next to me and flips through the channels, finally deciding on a program on Animal Channel about predators.

2011 (BEGINNING 1987)

COMUNEROS

The measure of a man is the depth of his convictions, the breadth of his interests and the height of his ideals.
- Anonymous

I've given up bugging Sonny about bolting down the driver seat in our dark-blue VW Beetle. The seat flies forward when I stop, slamming my chest into the steering wheel. Accelerating, the seat slides back, crushing tiny dangling legs behind. Why can't he fix this?

I'm irritable with these thoughts, as I pile the kids into the car and head for school. The road feels unusually bumpy and at the curved entrance ramp to the highway I lose control. We slip and slide until a bank of gravel at the edge of a deep ravine stops us. The kids, in spite of nonexistent seatbelts, are shaken but unharmed. I have four flat tires, six-inch slashes in each. While we slept, someone snuck onto our fenced-in property and did this!

I remember now. In the fading light of the previous

evening, three shadows had tapped with a key on our metal gate. From our terrace, twenty feet away, I had seen the same men chain-sawing old growth trees all afternoon on the property down the lane.

"We know you reported us to the authorities," the taller one had said.

"What are you..."

"Shut up, I'm talking. Do you know what the police did? They beat us up. And they wanted money. This is our land, and we can do with it as we please."

"But we need to take care of the forest for our kids and grandkids," I had said, trying to reason.

"The hell with our grandchildren," says the other. "If we don't cut, somebody else will, and if it's between the other guy and me making money, I'm going to take care of myself."

"Fine," I said. "Do what you have to do."

"We're warning you. Mind your own business."

I had thought that was the end of it.

Problems continue. Months later, I follow our wildly-barking dogs into our patch of forest to find three local women, who've jumped our chain-link fence, and climbed 15 feet high up into the giant pine trees. Their ankle-length, brilliantly-flowered skirts billow above me.

"What are you doing up there?" I say, dodging foot-long pinecones they're tossing. "I don't jump your fence and take your stuff,"

"This isn't your land," yells the largest. "This is a reservation. The mountain is ours!"

"I'm not going to argue," I say. "If you don't leave, I'm calling the police."

"Fucking bitch," one mumbles, as she struggles down through the branches.

Collecting mushrooms from the surrounding forest has been a tradition in the village for centuries. But now, with topsoil a major source of income, wild mushrooms are scarce. Soon the same three women are back, combing my little guarded forest for the precious spores.

"I already picked all the mushrooms," I say, dogs barking at the brazen trespassers.

"Well, we found some," the toothless hag hisses, throwing stones at the dogs.

I want to slap her

"What's that?" she asks, pointing to a wooden cross, *Descanse en Paz, Mimi* (Rest in Peace, Mimi) painted in black, dripping letters.

"It's a grave," I say, noticing the woman's eyes widening. "My friends buried their cat there. There are lots of graves in this wood. My mom is over there," I say, motioning to the foot of an oak tree. The ladies back away towards the entrance. I never see them again.

But their men return. One day we come home to find the western side of the cyclone fence ripped from the posts, bent up, a giant swath of forest floor stripped of life-sustaining topsoil.

A week later I'm on my way to the store, alone. Almost to the highway, where I'll make the 6-kilometer descent into Cuernavaca, I brake and the pedal slides to the floor with no resistance. I steer a sharp right into tall brush, and roll to a stop. There's no fluid in the slashed lines.

Twenty-five years ago, when we "bought" our two wooded acres, we didn't know that it was communal property, on a reservation. No one told us, not the lawyers who sold us our property, nor the government official who handed us the "legal" deed.

We make an appointment with the State Attorney for Land Issues. Maybe he can explain.

"Sorry to tell you, your house is on communal lands," the official says. "That deed isn't worth the paper it was issued on. Illegal to buy or sell."

In addition, since 1988 (we built in 1980) we are within the boundaries of a federal protected area: The Chichinautzin Biological Corridor, construction is now forbidden.

"Huitzilac is an autonomous village, like a country within a country," he says. "If you decide to stay, try to get along with the natives."

It's a free-for-all, *comuneros* grabbing as much land as money for fencing will allow, then "selling" their parcels by convincing unsuspecting outsiders that an official looking document guarantees them ownership.

Every few months machete-waving bands of 10 to 15 *comuneros* demand to see our papers. "We're taking your property if you don't have your documents in order," they threaten. Once, as they leave, screaming profanities, they spray paint the stone columns supporting the gate and bend six poles supporting the chain link fence.

We hear about families who return from a two-week vacation to find a family of *comuneros* living in their home, legally theirs now. It was abandoned.

Not long after my near fatal car accident, we read in the newspaper that two of the tire-slitting brothers are dead, killed in a shoot-out in front of city hall. Two other brothers are left: one in jail for kidnapping, and the fourth on the loose, still fencing in properties.

On a walk one day Sonny finds him deep in the forest, at it again:

"This tree's over three hundred years old," Sonny argues.

"If you bother us one more time, your kids are gonna look like those tires," he says, pointing his chain saw at Sonny's chest. "Or did you forget already?"

Around this same time, Mario, a local man who fixes my clogged drains, brings his six grandkids to join the Colibri Youth Orchestra. The tire slasher is the father of these talented, well-mannered kids. When I look for a new venue for rehearsals, this dad offers us his abandoned barn. The orchestra works a special magic in our community.

2012

AN AFFAIR REMEMBERED

The great enemy of the truth is very often not the lie -
deliberate, contrived and dishonest -but the myth -
persistent, persuasive and unrealistic. - John F. Kennedy

It's 2012 and what better place to be than Mexico, home of
the Mayans, whose ancestors predicted the world would
end, as we know it, on December 21st. Again, as at the
turn of the 21st century, people talk of computer systems
failing, the world shutting down. But I don't have to wait
until December for my world to crash.

   I'm at my desk, answering emails inquiring if Camerata
de Oro, our string quartet, is available for weddings in the
next few months. It's almost midnight and Sonny snores
from the loft area above. The business account is in
Sonny's name, but he never bothers with the internet.

   Then I see it: a friend request for Sonny.

   "Is that you, Rafael?" Maricela writes. "How've you
been all these years?"

   My God! I can't breathe. It's her. I thought the stake

I'd driven into the affair twenty years ago was the end of it. Sonny rustles awake. "Come to bed," he says.

Later, on my back, staring into the darkness, I whisper, "Sonny, you awake?"

"What is it?" he mumbles. "What's wrong?"

"Your old girlfriend. Maricela. She sent you a friend request."

"Tell her no," he says. "Take me off Facebook. I don't want anything to do with her!"

I sigh onto my side, the affair and pain of twenty years prior smothering again.

"You have nothing to worry about," he whispers into my back.

Tears drip onto my pillow.

Sonny thinks the crisis is over, but I'm curious. I need to know. Who is this woman who Sonny fell for? I ignore him and, a few days later, posing as my husband, accept her friend request. She answers right away asking, innocently enough, "How've you been?" Then, "I've missed you." And finally, "I've been with a man for six years, but I want to leave him. The only thing holding me back is our five-year-old son."

My head is spinning.

"Stay with his father," I type. "Kids need both parents"

"His father sits around and watches TV all day. I can't stand it."

"Don't take things so seriously."

Despite my lighthearted advice, I know what I'm doing is wrong.

"I've never forgotten you," she says. "You were everything to me. Such a great lover. I loved making it in the woods at your house."

The world is fading. I put my head down. Then, look up again at the screen.

"Let's meet for coffee. Would you like that?"

"I love my wife," I type. "It took a long time for her to trust me again."

"You told her about us?"

"Of course."

"When can I see you?"

"I can't," I write.

"It's just for coffee, silly."

Every time Maricela and I chat, my insides ache. Everything about this is sneaky-wicked. But she and Sonny had carried on behind my back for almost a year. It will take a lot worse to outdo their deceit.

Nevertheless, my conscience finally wins out and I tell Sonny what I've been up to. "Now she wants to meet up," I say.

He laughs, "Now she's falling for you!"

All these years I had fantasized that perhaps Sonny had made up the affair to lure me back to Mexico. But she exists. It happened. Pain, illogical and consuming, chokes all joy from my life. I want to run and never look back. Close the book on that life and slip it on the top shelf, between the photo albums, stuffed with thirty-five years of memories.

About the same time, a yoga-meditation-vegetarian retreat advertised on the community website catches my eye. Maybe this will help, maybe we can reconnect on a spiritual level.

We drive out past Tepoztlán, into the desolate, cactus-dotted country. The minute we pull up to the hotel lobby I realize there's more to this retreat than advertised. Men and women wander around in bright orange robes and turbans. They worship a deceased guru with a name I can't pronounce let alone remember. We're uncomfortable with the expectation that by the end of the retreat we will embrace the guru in the picture on the altar as our personal guide. I'm enveloped in despair, but Sonny carries me through meditations and workshops to the end of the retreat.

The following weeks, Sonny and I continue to meditate; it's the only time I feel a glimmer of peace. Sonny holds me, takes me out to candlelit dinners, reads me poetry. Nothing helps. I drag through every day praying this despair will pass, that soon I'll be whole again.

In September, still tormented by the reappearance of Sonny's lover, I register for another autobiography workshop with Citlali. Writing is therapeutic and my classmates are nonjudgmental and supportive. At the second class, I sob through the chapter on the affair and the new development.

"For God's sake," Israel, the only male in the class, says. "He was offered free sex whenever he wanted from a girl twenty years younger. What man wouldn't fall for that?"

"He's with you now," Citlali says, breathing the words. "For the last twenty years he says he's been faithful. What's the problem?"

"I know what it's like," Luisa says. "Laurie can't trust him."

"You guys need therapy," Israel says. "I know just the person. My wife cheated on me and if it weren't for this guy, I probably would have killed myself."

The lights are on in Sonny's shop when I arrive home. In the moonlight I stumble up the overgrown path. Sonny barely looks up, as I drop into a plastic chair next to the waist-high workbench. Bows with broken hair hang from nails in front of lattice windows, awaiting his expert hand. He's concentrated on clamping together the ribs of a double bass.

"I just can't go on like this," I say.

"What's wrong?" he says, turning.

"Your girlfriend," I say, throat tight. "I was going to suggest therapy, but what for?"

"I want us to work," he says. "Let's go."

Desperate for relief, I make an appointment.

Carlos, the therapist, meets us at the door. He's my height, dark skinned, jet-black hair. Jesus comes to mind. I sense Sonny's hesitation as Carlos ushers us through a fragrant, bougainvillea-blaring-magenta garden, around a swimming pool, into a small apartment, three plastic chairs set up in a tiny living-room.

Carlos asks why we're here. I try to explain, in an hour, our 35-year marriage, stressing that I can't process Sonny's affair sufficiently to reestablish a healthy relationship.

"I can give you the tools to stay together or to break up amicably," he says. "You will have to decide, and after a few sessions you'll know what to do."

We're here because we want to stay together. Isn't that obvious?

He continues with a Bible story: "Jesus became Divine because of treason," he says, looking directly at me. "The kiss in the garden."

I've never thought adultery could lead to enlightenment.

A glimmer of hope.

"We're brought up with cultural and religious beliefs, which have no basis in reality," he says. "Children use fantasy, make-believe, to process their world. Adolescents accept beliefs that adults stuff into their heads. Like, you go to college, you'll get a good job or, someday you'll find the perfect faithful partner. Then, as adults, life teaches us the truth. Infidelity. It happens. Often. But it doesn't mean love is dead or a marriage is over."

I'm obsessed with grief, mourning the death of a relationship, of a belief system.

"Death signifies change," Carlos says. "And change is good."

Carlos says our goal is to create a relationship of compassion and equality. He suggests *cinco minutos de la neta,* five minutes of truth, without interruption. Sonny begins. "I feel like you don't need me, I always worry you'll go on vacation and never come back...."

Then, my turn. "I feel like I'm not good enough. You looked for something better."

It's not helping. At our fourth session, I sit, bury my face in my hands and sob. Sonny and Carlos shift in their chairs and sigh.

"What are you feeling?" Carlos asks, after I empty my sorrow.

"I can't get over this. It's so stupid, but the pain. It's like I'm possessed."

"Does it feel like there's a wall you can't get past? Was there a tragic event in your childhood?"

I blow my nose and shiver. "Yes, my sister," I say. "She died."

"Can you share that?"

"She went off to her friend's birthday party, and never came back. They were at a swim club. No one was watching. She drowned." I cough, stare at the floor. "I was four years old. My 8-year-old sister cornered me, shook my shoulders, said I was never to say her name again. Ever. I was sure it was my fault, since my parents wouldn't talk about her either."

"You had nothing to do with it," Carlos says. "You were a baby."

"What can I do?" I ask. "Give me something concrete."

"Your sister went to a party," Carlos says. "Sonny was partying. You associate parties with death and guilt. With loss. Roxy's death was not your fault and Sonny's choices are not your fault. You need to face the misinterpreted childhood experiences you've buried and carried all your life. Say it. Connect with your subconscious."

I do what Carlos recommends and, like a miracle, a veil lifts. I'm back. I'm myself without the weight of grief. Will it trap me again as soon as we leave the office? But it lasts. It's not my fault. I'm good enough. I'm healed.

2012

MOURNING A VIOLIN

Be the reason someone believes in the goodness of people.
- Karen Salmansohn

The minute I set my suitcase and laptop down in my son Pete's house, I know something is missing. "My violin," I yell. "I left it on the bus!"

I fumble with my phone to find the number to the station. The bus, with my stowaway instrument, will take another half hour to get to the main station in downtown Puebla.

The woman who answers says she'll do her best to locate the violin but can't guarantee anything. I'm on my way, I say.

The GPS directs me to a tiny station in a run-down section of town. I race in.

"It's like losing a child," I say to the lady at the counter.

She calls the main station, then shakes her head. "Sorry. Nothing's been turned in. You'll need to go and look at the videos to see who got off with it."

It's dark now and I don't turn where I should. "Make a U-turn, make a U-turn, make a U-turn," says the nag on the phone. "Shut up, bitch!" I say.

Finally, I arrive at Grand Central Terminal, miss the entrance to the parking lot, and pull into a space in front of boarded up apartments. A homeless man with a long matted beard sits cross legged on cardboard, staring into my headlights, shaking his head.

I race into the station and ask a man in company uniform pacing and smoking a cigarette near the docked buses of Oro Lines. "Where's lost and found?"

"Right there," he says, pointing to a tiny office. "Closed. Opens at 6:00 AM tomorrow."

My eyes sting and I blink through tears, struggling to find my way home.

I set the alarm for 5:00 AM and try to sleep, but there will be no rest tonight. I stare into the darkness, my mind racing, my heart in pieces.

It's gone. I must accept it. Someone stole it off the bus. I'll never find them. The bus company keeps no record of passengers. The thief might try to sell it at a pawn shop. I'll call all the shops in Puebla, in the country. I'll put a notice on the internet to all my musician friends. But it has no luthier's tag inside, nothing to distinguish it, except for the blue case. I'm carving my initials into the ribs if I get it back. I could hang posters at the bus stations in Cuernavaca and Puebla. I'll offer a reward. I can never tell Sonny. But I've never lied to him. I could pray, but for a violin? Please God, let the best in people prevail. I picture a poor farmer opening the blue case to a wide-eyed eight-year-old potential virtuoso. You need to let go of material things, get back to meditating every day. I have no right to own this priceless jewel, taken from a victim of Nazi Germany, smuggled to England, and then brought to Mexico by a friend.

At 4:30, my brain still churning, I turn off the alarm, drag a comb through my hair, and set off. Roads are empty, except for some drunk teenagers who almost sideswipe me. That's lucky, I think.

At the freight office I explain to the man in charge.

"It's not the company's responsibility to look out for forgotten items," he says.

"I know that," I say, sleep-deprived edgy. "I was hoping someone had turned it in."

"You're in luck because we did find it," he says.

I cry out and reach for a chair, eyes filling with tears.

"Please, Señora, sit down," he says, taking my elbow and guiding me into the chair.

I cover my face and sob while he retrieves my treasure. I want to hug this stranger, smother his face in kisses, but I embrace the instrument instead. He asks for an ID, then tells me to sign papers. I dig in my pockets and hand him all the loose change I find.

2013

AN ORGAN LESSON

Ego trip: a journey to nowhere. - Robert Half

I'm thrilled when called to substitute as organist at Saint
Michael's Anglican Church in Cuernavaca, but this time
"there's just one small detail," the minister says. "You
can't touch the new organ." Those are the instructions
from Ana, the regular organist. I'll need to take my
keyboard.

"I'll let you know," I say. "Let me check my schedule."
I hang up and run to tell Sonny. "They hire me to be the
organist but won't let me play the organ!" I say. "I'm not
going."

"Are they paying you?" he asks.

I nod.

"Just shove that ego back down and do it."

Except for clicking from some of the keys, and a pedal
sticking occasionally, I thought the old organ was fine.
But Ana nagged for a new model, finally getting her 3
keyboard, hundred digitized stops, $70,000 dream

instrument.

Early Sunday, my heels echoing through the empty sanctuary, I drag my keyboard up to the loft at the rear of the church. There she stands, "My Queen," in all her untouchable grandeur. I brush past, bitter that I'm not deemed worthy enough.

I program Organ 1, a robust pipe organ, into the 7-octave keyboard and maximize the volume setting. My prelude and postludes are jubilant Bach fugues, and I clip through the hymns with joyous abandon.

During announcements, at the minister's prompt, all turn to me and wave a "thank you for coming." After church, the faithful shuffle into the fellowship hall for coffee and cookies. Soon a crowd surrounds me jibber-jabbering about how the new organ infuses a sense of exhilaration into the congregation. "I'm so glad we got that new organ!" "It sounds fantastic!" "That new organ just makes all the difference!"

How can I tell them that I played on a $186 Casio keyboard. What if the donor is in the group? I say nothing.

A month later a new minister is hired. "Can you substitute this week?" she says, over the phone. I ask if I can play the church organ. "Of course you can!" she says. "Nobody owns that organ!"

I tell her I'll need to practice, and she agrees. Now I have the keys to the church and to the organ and can attend to my Queen any time.

2013

A LIFE ERASED

The wound is the place where the light enters. - Rumi

All my life I've dreamed of making a pilgrimage to Cali, Colombia, the sacred place where we left my sister a nightmare ago. Sonny, my husband, is hesitant to spend the money. So, he'll be alone. Insecurities about our marriage circle in my brain like vultures over roadkill. Back to therapy.

Around and around we go in the session. I still have anxiety about our relationship, we´ll never be close again, I'll never find closure.   And then, my subconscious grabs the microphone: "You said once that, because we were never married in a spiritual ceremony, we weren't really married."

The therapist raises his eyebrows, let's out a long sigh and turns to Sonny.

"What's the problem with getting married? Afraid of commitment? After 35 years?"

"I have no problem with it," Sonny says. "I didn't know

it bothered her so much."

"I think it'd be a good idea for you to have a spiritual

LAURIE, ROXANNE, CHRISTIE, ANA

ceremony," Carlos says. "We're brought up with traditions, they're part of our culture. Confirm your spiritual commitment to one another. And do it before Laurie goes to Cali."

His promise will have to suffice because our son Pete, now 33 years old, surprises me with tickets for the two of us to fly to Cali in March. It's too soon to plan our sacred ceremony the way I want it. My own demons of guilt over my sister's death need resolution first. The wedding will have to wait.

My father's reluctance to discuss the Colombia chapter

of our lives makes it difficult to plan the trip.

"Why are you doing this to me?" he says over the phone, when I ask about names and places. "It's so painful, like it happened yesterday." I lost a sister, he lost a life.

I want to visit the institute, where my father taught English, our old house, and the cemetery where they left Roxy behind.

Finally, a call from Dad with a name: Reverend José Fajardo, a Presbyterian minister. "His sermon at Roxy's funeral service wrapped our bleeding hearts in hope," he says. Heart racing, I type his name into an internet search and find an obituary in Waxahachie, Texas for Fanny Fajardo, wife of a Reverend José Fajardo...lived in Cali....1960. They had four kids, one now a podiatrist in Texas. I call his office.

"I can't believe this," he says, after I tell him my story. "How did you find me?"

Then, the first of many disappointments. "My dad is in a convalescent home. He's 99 years old, not lucid enough to talk."

"So sorry," I say, my voice breaking.

He senses my disappointment and offers me the phone number of Carmen Rodriguez, a 60-year member of the church my family attended in Cali. "She'll be glad to show you around," he says. "I'll let her know you're going."

My sister Ana finds a file at my dad's house with letters from Colombia that my mother wrote to my grandmother; stories about a difficult, surreal life in a foreign land fill the pages. But the return address on the air mail envelopes is a post office box. No address. How will I find the house?

We land in a lush, emerald-green, overcast Colombia. It's comforting to travel with Pete; he doesn't mention my tears as we breeze through the airport in Cali. I can only think about how painful my parent's departure was 53 years earlier. I ache for them, for all of us.

The taxi drops us at the front door of our hotel, the Torre Cali, the tallest building in the city, guards with explosive-sniffing dogs at the entrance. The elevator opens on the 22nd floor. I gaze in awe as I enter our corner room. Instead of walls, two huge windows meet at the south-west corner. Out the right window lies our old neighborhood, banked up against the mountains.

It's a six-block hike to the Instituto Colombo Americano. We pass three-story Spanish-colonial houses, exactly like the watercolors hanging above the fireplace of my childhood home. But at the address I have for the Institute stands a modern, 20th-century cement monstrosity. I brush past swarming students, and we stop at the information desk.

"My dad used to be the director here," I say. "Could we take a look around?"

The receptionist opens a yearbook from 1960: Harold Saunders, Director 1959-1960. "Didn't stay long," she says. "I wonder why."

Arriving back at the hotel we find an email from my sister, Ana: "I asked George and Henry what address is on their birth certificates. I think we've got the house!"

I can barely breathe, the air weighs heavy humid. Faster, go faster, I think, as the taxi weaves through my old neighborhood. We stop in front of a giant electrical relay station.

"This is it. The address you gave would be here: Avenue 7, 27 North 123," the driver says.

"It can't be!" I say. "It's gone!" We get out and approach the fence. Behind the high power wires a dirt road winds up the hill.

"Yes, I remember, that's where we hiked to go butterfly hunting with my dad." He mounted the iridescent blue ones in big glass cases: one of the seven marvels of our neighborhood. My throat tightens, tears again.

"Things change, Mom," Pete says. "It's been over 50 years!"

"It's gone. All of it. Our lives, erased forever."

I call Carmen, the woman from the church who agreed to help us.

"I'd love to take you around to the cemetery on Saturday," she says.

"What cemetery?" I ask. "What's the name?"

"It'd be the Evangelical Cemetery. We're Presbyterian. The Catholics won't let us into their cemetery." she says. "They think we're heathens."

But I can't wait another day to visit the cemetery; I've waited 52 years.

The taxi driver drops us at the black wrought-iron gate. Rows and rows of dirty, water-stained 12" x 12" cement boxes stacked 8-feet high are crammed into a plot of land the size of a football field. A lone tree shades a cement bench on a grassy patch in the center.

"Maybe this isn't the place," I say.

"It's the only Evangelical cemetery in Cali," Pete says.

Finally the caretaker arrives, an old, hunched-over

PETE, EVANGELICAL CEMETERY, CALI,
COLOMBIA

hobbler, cold and indifferent when I tell him how many
years I've been away.

"If you don't pay your monthly fee, then we take the
bones out and put them in a common grave, over there," he
says, pointing to the back of the lot. "If you're all paid up,
then after four years we take you out and put you into a
little urn in one of those smaller squares up on top," he
says, nodding to the back wall.

I'm looking for my sister's grave, not shopping for
shoes. His indifference is irreverent.

The oldest boxes date back to 1967, seven years after

Roxy died. I read every crudely sketched name on the boxes anyway. She's not here. Her soul moved on years ago. Get a hold of yourself! Pete waits in patient silence as I walk up and down each row. Plastic flowers in cheap ceramic vases are thick with dust, gaudy black ribbons flap in the breeze, a tiny sparrow sits on a nest behind a chipped protective glass on the front of one of the boxes. Life in death. Finally, tears dripping from my cheeks, I sob into Pete's chest as he holds me. "I'm too late."

Back at the hotel, Pete and I each have a double bed in a room the size of a classroom. We fall asleep with the curtains open, the sprawling city twinkling below.

The sun's rays are just creeping over the mountains when I open my eyes. On the ridge a few miles away the Cristo Rey statue is gleaming. I'm four years old again. My sisters and I bounce around in the backseat of a 1950 blue Chevy. The winding road and gas fumes make me sick and we stop on the side of a desolate dusty road so I can vomit. Back in the car, Mom holds me and sings softly. Then, we're standing next to Christ's granite feet, huge as my legs. Who is this man? I wonder as I gaze up at his outstretched arms 80 feet above.

On Saturday, Carmen from the church, picks us up at the hotel. She's an intrepid driver, swerving in and out of traffic, barely missing jaywalking pedestrians. "Yes, I remember your sister's death," she says. "Your parents were so young. Tragic"

Our first stop is the cemetery, and I hope that yesterday we'd visited the wrong place. But Carmen stops in front of the same gate. She must be mistaken. No, Carmen is sure.

"In 1960 these structures weren't here," she says, waving at the boxes. "Your sister would've been buried here, in this grassy patch where this tree is now." She sees my tears and tries to comfort me, but I'm overcome by sadness, caught and twisted in my throat.

Pete sits reading a newspaper under the tree, and this time Carmen walks with me. We don't find Roxy.

Then we're off to Club San Fernando, which spans a whole city block. The entrance is boarded up but peeking through the cracks I see bulldozers pushing earth. I yell to the guard, and he opens the door a crack.

"Please," I say. "Please let me in. My sister drowned here years ago."

The place looks like it's been abandoned since the day of the tragedy. Weeds are knee deep, a kid's pool with two cement slides winding down into the middle is the only structure left. I look up at thick-trunked trees. "You know what happened." A chilly wind blows through the boughs and scatters trash.

Directly across the four-lane highway from the club looms the hospital where Roxy died and, 10 months later, where my brother was born. We take pictures. I'm wrapped in sorrow, grasping for memories, refusing to let her go.

The next day, I crisscross the city, hiking from government buildings to newspaper offices to finally, the basement of the National Library where I find newspapers from February 1960. The receptionist hands me surgery gloves and a mask. I imagine it's to protect the fragile precious archives. "It's dangerous to breathe the mold on the paper," she says.

Pereció una Niña en Club Campestre

La niña Rosanne Sanders, hija del profesor Harold Sander, director del Instituto Colombo-Británico, se ahogó en la piscina del Club Campestre en la tarde de ayer.

La niña se arrimó a la piscina, parece que sufrió un síncope, cayó al agua y, cuando sus padres se dieron cuenta, ya era tarde.

GIRL DROWNS IN POOL AT CLUB CAMPESTRE

Ahogada una Niña en la Piscina del "Club Campestre" de Cali

Roxanne Saunders, una niña de seis años de edad, hija de padres norteamericanos, murió ayer en forma dolorosamente trágica. Se ahogó en la piscina del "Club Campestre" en las horas de la tarde.

Roxanne alcanzó a ser rescatada con vida de las aguas de la piscina, pero al llegar al Hospital Departamental Universitario a donde fue conducida en busca de auxiliarla con oxígeno, falleció.

Era hija del señor Harold Saunders, director del Instituto Colombo-Americano y su señora esposa, Felisa de Saunders. Roxanne estudiaba en el Colegio Bolívar. La niña había sido llevada al "Club Campestre" por el señor Allim Johnson y sus hijos, a una fiesta familiar.

El inspector de permanencia sur, Hernando Jiménez, con la asesoría de su secretario, Rafael Álvarez, efectuó la diligencia legal del levantamiento del cadáver de la niña, conducido luego a la morgue del mismo Hospital Departamental, para ser necropsiado.

Muchos miembros de la colonia norteamericana se han hecho presentes para exteriorizar a los Saunders el pesar por la sensible tragedia.

I find the announcement in two newspapers. El Relator is wrong about everything. Her name is misspelled (Rosanne), our last name is misspelled (Sanders), the place where my dad worked is wrong (Colombo Británico). The article says that she had fainted and fallen into the water. No one knows what happened. And that my parents were there. They weren't there. She was with her best friend and family. The newspaper didn't even care enough to get the facts straight.

I rehang the newspaper on the wooden rack, walk to a table at the back of the bookshelves, sit and sob into my arms on the table. Our life here is gone. Erased. Except for Roxy. She will live as long as I do.

That evening, I watch the sun sink behind the mountain, red-orange streaks in the sky. I know why I'm here, what I've needed to say. "I would have saved you, even taken your place, if I could have," I say. "They couldn't bear the nightmare of your name, but I never forgot you, Rox."

2013

THE WEDDING

Life is a daring adventure or nothing at all.   - Helen Keller

The Mexican Post won't deliver the invitations to the US in time for our wedding, so I send them by email. My sisters and brothers think it's a joke and no one replies. But this is for real.

I plan meticulously for this milestone. First, I hire Vanessa to cater the five-course banquet. She'll bring tables and chairs, arrange them around the oak tree in the center of our stone, circular driveway, set them with bone china and crystal, hire waiters and bartenders. Danny and Beto will set up their DJ table, disco lights and sound equipment at the far end of the rented wood dance floor. Ceci, Pete's wife, will make the candlelit, floral centerpieces.

I buy a strapless, cream-colored floor-length dress with light-blue embroidered swallows down the front and Sonny buys two gold bands. What could go wrong.

The ceremony is scheduled for 2 o'clock. Friends, orchestra colleagues, Sonny's cousins, Roxy and Danny, all arrive before the hour. Except for Pete and family. *I will not let this stress me.*

DANNY, PASTOR GREG, SONNY, LAURIE

It's 2:30; some guests have been waiting an hour. We´ll just have to start without Pete.

Pine trees shade rows of chairs set up next to the bubbling brook in the garden. Sonny and I enter arm-in-arm and take seats facing the guests next to Pastor Greg, my pond behind us. Then, Pete breezes in with Ceci and year-old Rafa. I shake my head. He is late to everything. Sonny smiles and winks at me. All is well.

I can see the UNAM orchestra bass section in the last row, open rum and coke bottles propped against the legs of their chairs. *You better not touch those bottles again until the ceremony is over. I want this day to be perfect.*

Even though Roxy gave out colorful programs where it's explained, Pastor Greg invites friends and family to speak, if inspired, out of the meditative silence. I look out at familiar faces, special people I adore, and I'm overwhelmed with gratitude. Tears drip onto the program in my lap.

Then, bassist Joel is on his feet, interrupting my thoughts. His speech is slurred but his message poignant and sincere. My cheeks burn. I hope he doesn't tip over.

ROXY, SONNY, RAFA, LAURIE, PETE, CARMEN, DANIEL, CECI

"I look up to Laurie and Sonny. Their relationship is an inspiration to us all," he says. Soon, others follow and verbal gifts flow. A half hour later, our kids read inspirational quotes, and then Pastor Greg, from the Anglican, expat church in town, invites Sonny and me to stand. We vow to love one another unconditionally, and to cherish our differences. We exchange rings that will forever remind us of that promise. And then it's done. So far so good.

Waiters scurry to move the chairs to the banquet tables, champagne bubbles into glasses, and Pete stands to make a toast.

"To the best parents in the world."

As a gift to Sonny, I take the stage and, with Judith on the piano, I sing a parody of Gloria Gaynor's *I Will Survive*:

"…Thinking I could never live without you by my side,

And then I spent so many nights, thinking how these words were true

And then I knew, that there'd be no one else but you…"

It's in the wrong key for me, and I screech for the high notes. No one cares.

Sonny invites me for the first dance. Tells me he loves me. Hopes it'll last forever. Roxy performs an erotic fire show. The dance floor swells with laughter and love, Danny and Beto never missing a DJ beat. Mariachis arrive, with singing violins and blaring trumpets.

And then, my friend, Juana, whispers that the waiters are drunk.

"I'm not worried," I say, beaming over the joyous fracas. "Everyone celebrates tonight."

Love is not a fleeting, flimsy, wisp of desire, but a constant; as patient as we are undeserving. It's a decision to do what's right, to seek the Truth, and to commit unconditionally. And that, my friend, is why I stayed.

Acknowledgements

I would like to thank my teacher and editor, Laura Oliver, for sharing her wisdom in workshops and *The Story Within*. I am also grateful to Lyn Hopkins for meticulously converting my project into publishable format. Special gratitude to Daisy Willis, Andrea Saunders, Felice Hardy and Citlali Ferrer for their meticulous proof reading. Thanks to my writing group friends, Amy, Ruth, Betsy, Lyn and Esther for their enthusiasm and confidence, and to my siblings and parents, who suggested I write it all down. And finally, to my husband, kids and grandkids, thanks for fearlessly sharing the adventure.

Made in United States
Orlando, FL
26 March 2022

16156196R10183